SPACE HOPPERS

A fun-packed guide to travelling the solar system

with Space Cadets Dan and Steve

Mark Brake

MACMILLAN CHILDREN'S BOOKS

Thanks to Amanda Li, Dan Newman, Stuart Cox, John Piper and Jon Chase

First published 2010 by Macmillan Children's Books
a division of Macmillan Publishers Limited
20 New Wharf Road, London N1 9RR
Basingstoke and Oxford
Associated companies throughout the world
www.panmacmillan.com

ISBN 978-0-230-74833-0

This book is published to accompany the BBC Children's production *Space Hoppers* for CBBC,
produced by John Piper, Executive Producer Peter Davies,
starring Steve Marsh and Dan Wright, first broadcast in 2010.

A CIP catalogue record for this book is available from the British Library.

Typeset by Dan Newman
Printed and bound in China

Contents

INTRODUCTION

There are many worlds beyond this little planet we call home. And for many centuries we have gazed up at the sky, wondering what they might be like. But only recently have we begun to find answers. We have started to explore our solar system, sending astronauts to the Moon and robotic spacecraft into deeper space.

The cosmic neighbourhood we have discovered has helped us transform dozens of planets and moons from mysterious dots of light into real worlds, each with its own unique climate and history.

We have an urge to explore. To travel to new places, to cross that canyon, to climb that crater, to set foot on that new world. Only a lucky few have travelled from the blue into the black, and even fewer (twelve, to be precise) have left their footprints on another world. Maybe one day you will follow them – perhaps you will walk on Mars, take a ride in a rocket, or look back at the Earth from the depths of space.

To find out more about what it would be like to travel in space, join the Space Hoppers on their quest to explore the unexplored.

GREETINGS, SPACE CADETS!

Forget Greek island hopping. That's so over. **Space Hopping** is where it's at.

After all, this is the 21st century – and when space tourism finally becomes a reality, you can be sure that the pair of us, Dan and Steve – Space Cadets extraordinary – will be ready.

If, like us, you want to find the best places to visit on space vacation, you've picked up the right book.

So stop mucking up the lovely clean pages with your grubby fingers, get over to the cash desk and say these magic words: 'Space is ace and that's why I would like to purchase this fun and fact-packed volume.'

Done that? Good. We can begin.

You've signed up for the ultimate space cruise. We're taking in blazingly hot destinations like the Sun, bone-numbingly cold destinations like Saturn, and the odd very bizarre place that manages to be blazingly hot and bone-numbingly cold at the same time.

Only the fearless need read on. Prepare to encounter amazing moons, storms that have been raging for hundreds of years, and even comets and asteroids that could be on a collision course with Earth.

Brace yourselves – things could get spacey.

VENUS! SATURN!! URANUS!!!
DANGEROUS!!!!

Steve and Dan,
Space Cadets

SPACE IN THE SUN

The first place on our solar system must-visit list has got to be the Sun. It's brilliant. Literally. OK, we know the Sun is way too hot for us to actually *visit* it. We'd get burned to pieces.

Besides, at 93 million miles away, it's a fair trek. Just imagine, you set off in one of those Harry Potter flying cars at 93 mph. Don't worry, there are no speeding laws in space, bar this one: nothing travels faster than the speed of light. But the Sun is so far away that even at 93 mph it would take you a million hours to get there!

But if we could reach the Sun, it would be well worth the trip. The Sun is the key to life on Earth, and key to any alien life in the solar system, if it's out there. In fact, the Sun drives everything that happens in the solar system, and how it all began is an incredible story.

Dan and Steve are hot on the trail of the sunniest spots in space. Will the intrepid Space Cadets be deterred by the scorching heat?

The Power of the Sun

Because the Sun rises every morning and sets every evening we maybe take it for granted, but we shouldn't. Because without it there would be no light, no heat, no food to eat, no weather, no days, no seasons, no Earth as we know it. In fact, no solar system at all.

To give you an idea of the sheer size of the Sun, you could fit one million Earths inside it. Or, to put it another way, if you wanted to fly right round it in a jumbo jet you would have to keep going non-stop for 227 days. Now that's a long-haul flight that would be no good for your carbon footprint!

And the Sun *is* unbelievably hot – giving off as much energy as 7 million million nuclear explosions every second.

It's amazing to think that this ball of fiery energy has been burning like this for five billion years. One day it will eventually die. But don't panic, that won't be for another five billion years.

So many stars . . .

Stars like the Sun power our entire universe. Scientists have found that there are more stars in space than there are grains of sand on all of the beaches on planet Earth! Imagine yourself on one of those beaches. You reach down, hands cupped, and gather up two handfuls of the golden sand. Then you let the sand fall through your fingers, the grains glistening as they catch the sunlight. Each grain is a star. And each star is a sun, like our own local star, the Sun. So much sand, so many stars.

> The sun is way too hot for us to visit. We'd get scorched into oblivion.

> Come on! There's no need to be so negative.

> And it would be worse for me. I'm *ginger.*

> Getting scorched into oblivion would be worse for you because you're ginger? Nonsense. It will all be a breeze as long as we set off at night, when it's a bit cooler.

> Oh yeah . . . Steve, are you sure that's right?

> On the glorious day that we head off on a sunny space vacation, everything is going to be just fine.

Hello, holidaymakers! Need help choosing which Sun-kissed space destination to visit? Well, this is the show for you: Spa-cation Spa-cation Spa-cation. The holiday show that really is out of this world!

Sunny Spa-cations

Death Valley, California – one of the hottest spots on planet Earth – a place where you can really appreciate the Sun's incredible power. But what else does our solar system have to offer?

① Planet **Mercury** is our first stop, with soaring temperatures of 426°C. Though it's not much of a party planet, since there's no atmosphere.

② Next stop is planet **Venus**, the satellite of love. The planet sparkles like a jewel in the canopy of the heavens, apparently. But on the surface, it's rough. At 461°C, Venus' temperature is hot enough to melt lead!

③ If a moon is more to your liking, then consider little **Io**, which orbits Jupiter. It may be a long way from that cruel old Sun, but Jupiter's gravity makes up for it. It pulls little Io about so much that it's littered with volcanic hot spots and temperatures of 1300°C.

④ And while we're in the Jupiter system, perhaps **Jupiter** itself is more to your taste? This failed star has a core hotness of 29726°C, though this is still pathetically small next to the centre of the Sun itself. (The king of the solar system has a core that comes in at a whopping 15.7 million°C.)

Hey, space travellers! Take your pick out of these planets in your lovely little solar system. But remember, while this shows the relative sizes of the planets, it doesn't show the real distances between them (see the chart on page 50). Some journeys will take so long that you'll be years older by the time you get there!

These planets do sound worryingly *hot*.

Certainly hotter than Filey promenade on a May Bank Holiday.

Maybe too hot for the likes of a fair-skinned ginger fella like me?

Oh, here we go again. Ginger, ginger, ginger. Why don't you get over yourself?

Neptune   Uranus   Saturn   Jupiter   Mars   Earth   Venus   Mercury

④   ③   ②   ①

SPACE IN THE SUN | **11**

Super Sun Facts

Average distance from Earth:
1.5 x 10¹¹ metres (93 million miles)

Average diameter: 109 Earths

Surface area: 11,990 Earths

Volume: 1,300,000 Earths

Temperature of surface: 5505°C

Temperature of core: 15.7 million °C

Luminosity: 3.846 x 10²⁶W (and you thought a 100 W light bulb was bright!)

Composition: 74% Hydrogen, 25% Helium, 1% everything else!

Time taken by the Sun for one complete orbit of centre of Milky Way: 250 million years

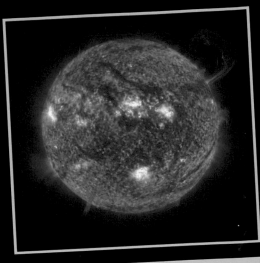

A photo taken on 14 September 1999 shows a huge handle-shaped cloud of dense plasma (super-hot gas) erupting from the Sun's atmosphere.

If the Sun was that big (on the left) the Earth would be about this big (above).

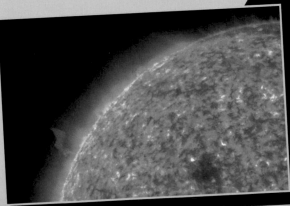

Using filters to block out a lot of the light, telescopes can see details of the surface of the Sun – which is surprisingly lumpy or 'granular'.

The creation of the Sun

What we think happened was that around 5 billion years ago, the Sun was a massive cloud of dust and gas. The cloud collapsed in on itself after being hit by the shock waves from a nearby exploding star.

Gravity forced all the gas tighter together, until it got so hot and tightly packed at the centre that something called nuclear fusion happened – sending massive amounts of energy outwards from the centre.

The power of gravity pressing inwards and the energy from the nuclear fusion pushing outwards balanced each other out and created a constant and stable energy-giving star, the Sun.

Sun Worshippers

The Sun is so important to life on Earth that human history is full of cultures that understood its life-giving powers.

Worship of the Sun was very common in Ancient **Egypt**, and the motion of the Sun across the sky had great significance for its people. In Ancient **Aztec** culture, their Sun god was thought to be the leader of all the heavens. And in **Chinese** culture they believed that ten sunbirds lived in the sky. The Chinese also believed that a solar eclipse happened when the dog of heaven bit off a piece of the Sun. It was quite common for Chinese people to hit pots and pans during an eclipse, to drive away the 'dog'.

Sun worshippers also lived in the British Isles. Dating of remains found at **Stonehenge** shows that burials took place there as early as 3000 BC. And while there is still some debate as to why Stonehenge was built, one thing seems clear. The monument is made to face the rising Sun on the midwinter solstice (the 'shortest day', the one with least daylight). Possibly those ancient worshippers felt the need to call the Sun back for another summer, to help grow crops.

Newgrange Passage Tomb in Ireland was built around the same time as Stonehenge. It was also built to face the rising Sun on the midwinter solstice, to allow sunlight to shine on the bones of the dead inside. It was thought this would help loved ones get an easy passage into the afterlife.

Above: Konark Temple in Orissa, India, built as a huge chariot for the Sun God Surya in the thirteenth century. The chariot is intricately carved, pulled by stone horses and guarded by two stone lions.

Below: A solar eclipse in 2006 as seen from Mt Elbrus in Russia.

Make a Solar-powered Oven

As you know, the Sun is the most powerful source of light and heat in our solar system. And now you can use the Sun's energy by trapping it in a box to make an 'oven'! But remember, you will need one very important thing for this experiment – a nice sunny day . . .

You will need:

- sunshine – don't try this on a cloudy day
- two takeaway cardboard pizza boxes – one large, one small
- tin foil
- marker pen
- newspaper
- scissors
- glue or sticky tape
- black paint and brush
- clingfilm
- a plate that will fit into the small pizza box
- something to cook in your oven – how about biscuits or small cakes? You can make your own mixture or get the ready-to-mix type in a box.

WARNING!
Don't try to cook any kind of meat or fish using this method as these foods must always be very well cooked before eating!

3 ...

4 ...

I know just the thing to keep you perky while your biscuits are cooking, Dan.

What?

How about . . . a little bit of rap with an underlying scientific message?

What, the gift of science from MC Orbit, wrapped up with rap? *Now* you're talking!

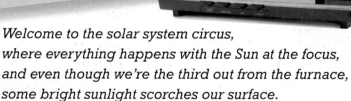

SUN RAP

Welcome to the solar system circus,
where everything happens with the Sun at the focus,
and even though we're the third out from the furnace,
some bright sunlight scorches our surface.

Earth gets energy as heat and light,
that's used by the plants and the rest of life,
and water is liquid, not steam or ice,
at 93 million miles; just right!

All over the world we have worshipped the Sun,
and looked at the place where it all began.
A total eclipse still amazes and stuns.
If you're caught in the shadow, you're the lucky ones.

The very large telescope helps us to peer
at distant stars that we can compare.
But our Sun could fit a million Earths in its sphere
While living for five more billion years.

TO COLDLY GO: ICE!

The universe is a place of unimaginable contrasts and extremes. Extreme distances, extreme atmospheres and, of course, extreme temperatures. And while we already know that some parts of our solar system are blisteringly hot, you might be surprised to find out that other parts are mind-numbingly cold.

The very coldest places in our solar system are to be found – you've guessed it – the furthest away from the sizzling Sun. Places like the dwarf planet Eris, chilly Triton – one of Neptune's moons – and icy Ganymede, the freezing moon of Jupiter. Scientists have also recently discovered that the centres of the dark craters at the south pole of the Moon are among the very coldest places ever recorded.

The high rims of the craters block the Sun out completely, keeping them at a constant temperature of –240°C. Compare this to the lowest temperature ever recorded on the Earth at –89°C in Antarctica. It's certainly chilly, but nothing compared to what lies out there for our intrepid Space Cadets.

Dan and Steve will need a lot more than central heating in their underwear when they set off on their icy adventure. And they soon discover that in space, no one can hear you freeze!

Brace yourself, Dan – things are about to get *nippy*!

Freezing Spa-cations

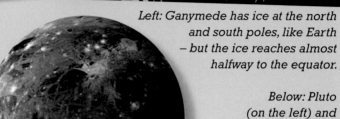

Left: Ganymede has ice at the north and south poles, like Earth – but the ice reaches almost halfway to the equator.

If getting up close and cuddly with an avalanche of snow and ice is your idea of holiday heaven, then look no further. Have we got sub-zero space destinations for you!

● First, check out the ultimate chill-out zone of **Ganymede** – the moon of Jupiter where the thermometer drops to –203°C. That's 186 degrees colder than your average freezer. Brrrr!

● Catch the cold of your life on **Triton** – the largest moon of Neptune. It was once thought to be the coldest place in the solar system at a teeth-chattering –235 °C.

● Freeze, suckers! You will on **Pluto** – a dwarf planet beyond Neptune. All the way down to –240 °C. So pack an extra pair of socks and knickers. Hey! Make that two pairs.

● And finally, for the ultimate winter wonderland, try the dwarf planet of **Eris** – the most distant object we've discovered in the solar system at a bone-numbing –243°C.

Below: Pluto (on the left) and its moon Charon, taken by the Hubble Space Telescope at a distance of 2.75 billion miles. That's like photographing a baseball from 40 miles away!

The Ice Men Cometh

Dan and Steve soon realize that if they are going on an ice vacation, they will need to get used to the cold. Fast. So they throw away their thermals and get close to some chilly stuff. After a day of sub-zero experimentation, things soon begin to cool off between the pair.

But there's one thing they eventually agree on – to try out a different destination. So off they coldly go … to the most picture-perfect destination of all: Saturn.

Sitting on a tray of ice cubes for two hours has really taught me a lot about winter space tourism.

So what *exactly* have you learned?

Cold stuff is *really horrible* and should be avoided if possible.

The Icy Rings of Saturn

Grumpy Galileo

Dan and Steve find Saturn a cold, unwelcoming place. It's −130°C, don't you know. But it is also surrounded by the most beautiful rings in the solar system.

These were first discovered in the early days of the telescope, around 400 years ago. Telescopes weren't up to much in those days, so famous Italian astronomer Galileo actually thought that Saturn had ears! He got even more confused when the ears seemed to disappear, then come back again. It made him very grumpy.

But in 1655, Dutch astronomer Christiaan Huygens got it right. He was the first person to describe the rings as a disc surrounding planet Saturn.

Since then, for many astronomers, Saturn has been the most fascinating of all the planets and its rings one of the true wonders of the solar system. In recent years we have been able to see them close up in incredible detail because of amazing robotic spacecraft that are constantly sending back new information.

One of these spacecraft, NASA's Cassini-Huygens probe, has been on a thirteen-year quest to find out more about Saturn and its many moons. Here are some of the incredible pictures it has sent back.

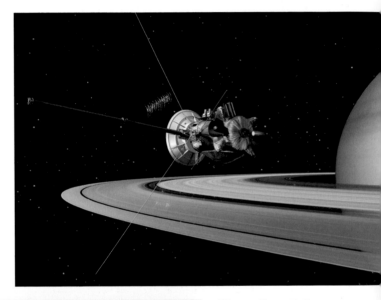

Above: An artist's impression of Cassini-Huygens approaching Saturn.

Left: Cassini captured Saturn and some of its fifty-plus moons from a distance of about 684,000 miles.

Above: Saturn's visible rings.

Left: The distance across the rings in this view is 124,000 miles. The tiny white dot at the bottom is the moon Atlas, 20 miles in diameter.

Made from a moon

So how were Saturn's beautiful rings first formed? Well, scientists believe that hundreds of millions of years ago there was another moon made of ice orbiting Saturn. This moon was smashed up, being either hit by an asteroid or ripped apart by the immense pull of gravity from the other moons and Saturn itself. (And if you think that's far-fetched, read about what happens to poor little Io in the next chapter!)

Anyhow, once the icy moon disintegrated, the shattered fragments began to orbit Saturn, and the rings were formed.

Even though the rings orbiting Saturn look pretty solid, they are in fact made up of lots of floating lumps of ice – very similar to icebergs on Earth – all orbiting the planet in a kind of slow-motion blizzard.

Most of these chunks of ice are no bigger than a centimetre across, although a few are the size of a house and others are as much as a kilometre wide.

Just imagine what it would be like sitting on an iceberg floating in orbit around Saturn. Now that would be awesome!

Hey Dan, what's the difference between an iceberg and a clothes brush?

One crushes boats, the other **brushes coats**! Good, huh?

I don't know, Steve. But I suspect you're going to tell me.

Freezing Volcanoes

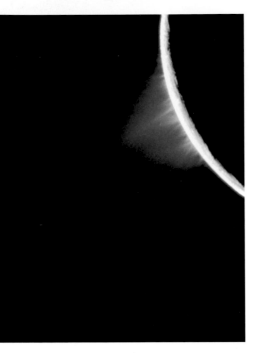

Oone last wonder of the Saturn system is the amazing icy world of Enceladus.

It's a moon orbiting about 870 million miles away from the Sun – which means it's seriously cold. We didn't know much about it until a few years ago when the Cassini mission flew just 50 metres above its surface. And the pictures it sent back blew scientists away.

It sounds like something out of science fiction, but even stranger. This is a world that should be frozen solid but whose surface is erupting with volcanoes. Except these volcanoes spit out not boiling hot lava … but freezing fountains of ice.

Here on Earth, heat below the surface creates geysers (below right), which launch jets of boiling water up into the sky. And we think something similar happens on Enceladus – except that once the water explodes through the surface, the frozen temperatures turn it straight away into ice. And because there is no gravity, the ice fountains then soar up to mind-blowing heights of over 60 miles, eventually joining the rings of Saturn.

With the Sun behind Enceladus, Cassini could see individual 'fountains' of ice.

The south polar region of Enceladus is striped with deep grooves, from which the jets emerge.

It's an amazing sight, but scientists have also got very excited about Enceladus because the mixture of heat, water and some of the chemicals Cassini has detected in the ice makes up the three main requirements for life.

In the search for life beyond Earth this small frozen moon was not high on anyone's list of places to look – but it could be that it's here that we find it.

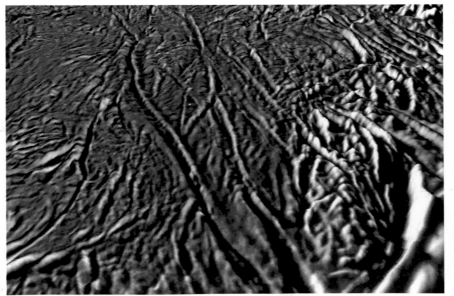

Ice Cubes Under Pressure

As you know, Saturn's rings are formed out of shattered pieces of ice, many of them no bigger than a centimetre across. These came from an ice moon which was destroyed by impact pressure. To show how ice reacts under pressure you can try these experiments.

You will need:

- ice cubes
- a length of fishing line or wire (not string)
- two heavy (but not too large) objects to use for weights, e.g. tins of beans or sweetcorn
- a container such as a flower pot – this needs to have quite high sides so that the weights are held up from the tray
- a tray to keep things from getting wet

At a much bigger level, the massive force of atmospheric pressure on some planets and moons makes ice melt. When it refreezes, a new, denser form of ice is created, the kind that scientists think may only exist in the interiors of frozen ice-moons that belong to the outer planets of our solar system.

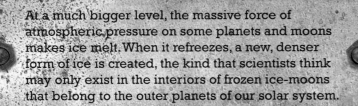

Hey, Dan, do you think we're as chillin' as MC Orbit?

Steve, after the icy experience we've had, **no one** could be cooler than us.

ICE RAP

The further we venture, the colder it seems,
Mars is much colder than Earth's ever been,
and Jupiter's biggest moon, called Ganymede,
is minus two hundred and three degrees.

Then Cassini went to the sixth planet Saturn,
a mission that's taken thirteen years to happen.
This gas planet doesn't have a surface to land on,
but its many rings form an interesting pattern.

They're made of chunks from an ice moon shattering.
Since then Saturn is the planet with the biggest bling.
But something amazing is still happening,
providing some ice for the outermost rings.

The moon Enceladus has heat that squeezes . . .
. . . out chemicals in water that quickly freezes.
These ice volcanoes have scientists very pleased,
because they seem to have all the things that life needs.

LOST IN LAVA

Explosive volcanic action has always been a big part of the history of our world – and it still is. On Earth at any one time there are likely to be as many as twenty volcanoes which are live, kicking, and actually erupting.

Volcanoes are openings in the surface of the Earth where pent-up hot gases from deep down rise up to heat the surface rock. The heat can be so immense that the rock turns into deadly liquid lava that flows from the top of the volcano during an eruption. Volcanic action is often accompanied by earthquakes and can have a massive and devastating effect on the environment.

A part of the world actually built by volcanoes is the Hawaiian Islands in the Central Pacific Ocean. Here you can see red-hot lava, brand new and still erupting today. If you stand just a few metres away, the scorching heat is almost unbearable. You could even take some bread along for instant toast!

But how do volcanoes in other parts of the solar system measure up to the ones we have here on Earth? Dan and Steve go with the flow as they head for the most explosive locations in space.

Explosive Spa-cation

Welcome back to Space Cadet Tours – the only holiday company that takes you to the most explosive spots in the universe! We always show you the biggest and the best – and today is no exception.

Olympus Mons

Once, Earth was the only planet that we knew for certain had volcanoes. But when we started to explore space we discovered that volcanoes existed on planets and moons right across the solar system. And now you can see them for yourselves, space travellers!

● First stop, **Mars**, the Red Planet. But be prepared, scientists think we will need eighteen months to make the trip. It will be well worth it, for Mars has the biggest volcano of all, **Olympus Mons**.

● This huge volcano, like many of those on Earth, has been slowly built upwards as layer after layer of lava has cooled down and turned into rock. In time, it has created this gently sloping, and largest mountain in the solar system. Olympus Mons is nearly three times taller than the biggest volcano on Hawaii.

Space probes and rovers investigating the Red Planet are constantly sending information about Mars back to Earth. None have spotted a volcanic eruption yet. But if you continue on our volcano-spotting vacation, you'll discover what's shaking some other planets . . .

Eighteen months for a trip to Mars and back? Wow! That's a long time.

I'd better cancel the newspapers. And let my mum know where I'm going.

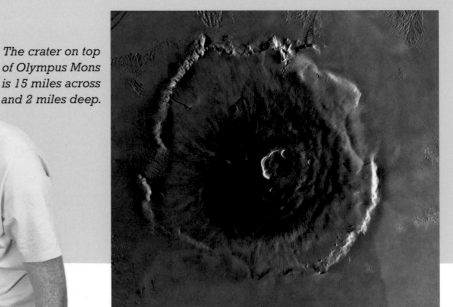

The crater on top of Olympus Mons is 15 miles across and 2 miles deep.

Volcanic Venus

Venus is the second nearest planet to the Sun and, other than our Moon, the brightest light in our night sky. But the thick blanket of clouds covering its surface meant that, until very recently, it remained a world of mystery.

When we finally managed to send crafts to Venus to look below the cloud cover, what we saw was lava – the kind of rock that is created by volcanoes – as far as the eye can see.

The big difference on Venus is that the lava rock is spread across the entire planet, created by over 55,000 separate volcanoes! Venus is a lava world, the volcano capital of the solar system, and the closest planet to hell that we have found so far.

Probes have not yet seen any volcanic eruptions on Venus. But they have detected the eggy smell of the volcanic gas sulphur in the planet's atmosphere, which could mean they are happening somewhere on the planet.

Above: Sapas Mons volcano on Venus is about 250 miles across.

Left: Venus is normally hidden by thick clouds; the Magellan probe's radar revealed the surface.

Below: Maat Mons is 5 miles high. Solidified lava in the foreground extends for hundreds of miles.

Sulphur? It smells like everyone in the world has farted at the same time!

I think, Dan, if we are to become the best Space Cadets ever, we are going to have to use our noses as well as our massive brains.

Incredible Io

Perhaps one of the most exciting volcano discoveries made was on **Io**, one of the many moons of **Jupiter**. Scientists were stunned when they saw amazing pictures beamed back of a live and active volcano named Pele spewing out lava for miles into space. Accompanying the lava were plumes of gas that were reaching as high as 185 miles above the little moon.

Amazingly, it turns out that all that massive volcano-making heat energy on Io is caused by a process that we take for granted here on Earth: the pull of gravity that causes tides.

On Earth, as the planet turns, the tides of the oceans go in and out. This is due to the pulling effect of the Moon's gravity. But on Io there is more than one competing pull of gravity, as it is being tugged both by Jupiter and by other moons like Europa and Ganymede.

All the different pulls on Io mean that something much more amazing happens than the ocean tides of Earth. There is no water on Io, so what happens is that the surface itself – made of solid rock – rises and falls by anything up to 100 metres.

This means that Io's shape is changing all the time, from a sphere to something more squashed and oval-shaped. And being squeezed in and out makes Io heat up. A lot.

It's the heat coming out of the volcanoes that makes the surface of Io look like a pizza planet. Wonder what it tastes like?

Above: the reddish ring of debris around Pele is 870 miles across – the distance from London to Rome.

Right: the plume of Pele erupts into space.

A planet covered in zits where your house moves around?

Whoa! No thanks, matey!

Right: an active eruption of lava, about 30 miles wide, seen by the Galileo spacecraft in 2000.

Eruptions on Earth

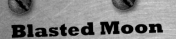

Earth is teeming with volcanoes. Just for starters, there's Mount Stromboli in Europe, Mount Fuji in Japan and Erta Ale in Ethiopia, East Africa – one of the most hostile places on Earth. The name Erta Ale means 'smoking mountain' but that hardly does it justice. The awful heat. The overpowering smell of sulphur from the rocks. It's like hell on Earth. In fact, one of Erta Ale's ancient names was 'the gateway to Hell'! Its last major eruption was in 2005. And the effects of a volcanic eruption can be devastating.

● In 1980, a volcano called **Mount St Helens** in Washington in the United States erupted unexpectedly. As the trapped gases under the rock were released, a massive explosion blew the top clean off the mountain. Ash clouds shot up 12 miles high, and mud slides and avalanches crashed down the mountainside. The eruption killed 57 people and destroyed many homes.

● Even worse was the 1991 eruption of **Mount Pinatubo** in the Philippines. This was the second biggest eruption of the twentieth century (the largest ever was Krakatoa in 1912). Unsurprisingly, the area around the volcano was devastated but this explosion had a global impact too. It threw out 10 billion tonnes of magma and forced huge amounts of aerosols (tiny particles) into the stratosphere. A haze of sulphuric acid formed, which lowered the world's climate by 0.5°C. Luckily, scientists forecast the eruption and at least 5,000 lives were saved.

Blasted Moon

Even our Moon gets a piece of the volcanic action. Astronauts once brought back samples of Moon rock that had been formed by volcanoes. And scientists and astronomers still dream that one day it will be possible for space travellers to see the effects of volcanoes on a planet like Mars for themselves.

Above: Cleveland Volcano in Alaska 2006, photographed from the International Space Station.

Below left: Mount Pinatubo erupts in 1991.

Below: Mount St Helens literally blew its top – before and after May 1980.

Make an Exploding Volcano

An erupting volcano must be one of the world's most exciting – and dangerous – sights! Now you can create your own realistic eruption at home. Sit back, and watch the lava flow!

You will need:

- modelling clay
- a tray or large plate
- the inside of a toilet roll
- paint and brushes
- a heaped teaspoon of bicarbonate of soda
- 30ml vinegar
- food colouring – this is optional but gives a spectacular effect, particularly in red or yellow

VOLCANO RAP

When rocks get too hot they turn into magma . . .
. . . underground, but on the surface it's lava.
When it cools down then the layers get harder,
forming land or volcanoes after.

An eruption occurs just like a fountain.
Check out the gases and rocks it's spouting.

But it's not just Earth where this has happened.
Let's make moves to Mars to the most massive mountain,
Olympus Mons, the solar system's biggest,
seventeen miles; three times Everest.

Think that it's active? Come on, take a better guess.
If you want activity remember Io's pizza face,
its tidal forces! Ring a bell?
But for the most volcanoes, look closer still,
on Venus where there is more to tell,
as long as you can cope with the sulphur smell.

DON'T KNOCK THE ROCK

We know about the eight planets: Mercury, Venus, Earth, Mars, Jupiter, Saturn, Uranus and Neptune. But that's not all there is to the solar system. There's all sorts of other stuff out there, whizzing in high-speed orbit round the Sun, from the lumps of ice that make up the spectacular rings of Saturn to huge rocky asteroids and frozen comets.

Comets and asteroids are the building blocks of the solar system. They are the leftover bits from the stuff that made all the planets. Comets are made from ice and dirt, and asteroids are huge lumps of rock and metal.

Comets are like dirty snowballs, a mad mixture of rock and ice. They come in all sizes, ranging from only half a mile to tens of miles across, and have incredibly long tails that can stretch hundreds of millions of miles through space.

Asteroids are mostly to be found in the big gap between Mars and Jupiter called the asteroid belt. But the home of comets is the mysterious back of beyond. Comets hail from faraway zones like the Kuiper belt beyond Neptune, and the mysterious Oort Cloud. No one has actually seen this Oort Cloud. It sounds like a baddy from Dr Who, but we think it is beyond the outer limits of the solar system. Dan and Steve are about to investigate . . .

What would happen if any of this stuff was to crash into Earth?

It says in 'The Cadet's Guide' that a layer of gas around the Earth called the atmosphere burns up most comets and asteroids.

Phew!

Greetings, thrillseekers! No holiday in the solar system would be complete without trekking on the trails of comets and asteroids. Today the solar system will be your galactic theme park and riding a comet will be the best white-knuckle ride you could ever experience!

Zooming Spa-cations

Meteor Crater in Arizona.

Comets wing their way to the Sun from the outer limits of the solar system. So you will catch a ride through interplanetary space, whizz round the Sun like a slingshot, catch a few rays, then shoot back again, rattling out through the solar neighbourhood. Your solar circuit is complete!

If you're up for an even bumpier ride, then there's no more extreme sport than navigating your way through the asteroid belt!

Steve is up for it. Not only is he a bit of a thrillseeker, he's got a new sat nav he wants to try out. Dan isn't quite so sure. But they will both need to keep their wits about them if they're going to avoid crashing into one of the tens of thousands of asteroids out there.

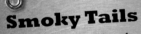

Smoky Tails

Comets' tails look colossal but in fact they are nature's most spectacular use of the smallest amount of material. Close up, a comet's tail is the same consistency as smoke. If you managed to collect it all up, it would probably fit into a suitcase!

You can risk your life if you like. You'll find me feeding the ducks and having a punt round the boating lake.

Don't be such a wuss. To trek through the solar system on the trail of an asteroid, we need to be **fearless**.

I **am** fearless. Just not when it comes to frightening stuff.

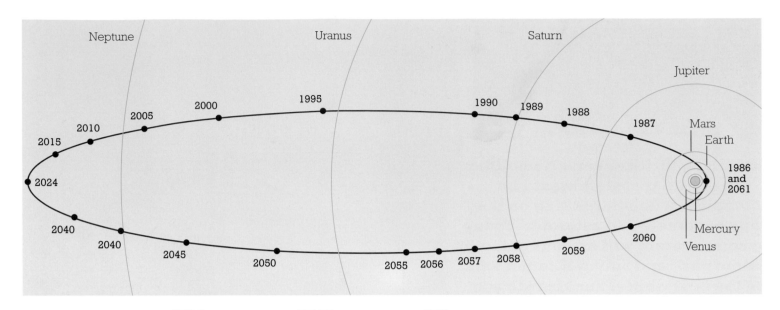

Know Your Comets

The diagram shows the orbit of Halley's Comet, the most famous comet of all time. You'll see where its orbit (in pink) meets the orbit of all the planets in our solar system (in blue). You can see that Halley's Comet last came shooting past Earth in 1986 – but don't worry, you'll have your chance to view this amazing sight in 2061. One to look out for when you're old and grey!

Below: Edmond Halley worked out from historical records that a comet seen in 1607 was the same as one seen in 1531. He predicted it would return in 1758. Now named Halley's Comet, people have been spotting this comet since at least 240BC – including this instance recorded on the Bayeux Tapestry.

Thought you knew all about comets? No? Then read on.

● We believe the main **home** of comets is believed to be the Oort Cloud, a vast spherical shell of comets 1,000 times as far out as the distant Pluto. The cloud may have as many as 1 trillion (that's a million million!) comets.

● The planets of the solar system have circle-shaped, or elliptical, orbits. Comets have more cigar-shaped, or parabolic, orbits. The planets all orbit the Sun in the same flat plane, but comets can come winging in from any direction, all 360 degrees!

● Some comets get so close they are called **Sun-grazers**. Others get so close they smash into the Sun, never to return home!

● Comets can weigh from 10 million to 10 trillion tonnes – which is pretty tiny, in space terms. (You'd need 70 million large comets to equal the mass of Earth's Moon!)

● We can predict when some comets will come into view. **Short-period** comets return often. Halley's comet, for example, has a period of 76 years – which means it has been spotted from Earth every 76 years or so. **Long-period** comets return rarely, and have periods of thousands of years. So far, we've only spotted about 3,648 comets. 400 of these are short-period and 1,500 are Sun-grazers.

How to Bend Space – with a Duvet!

Great comets

What makes a comet 'great'? A number of things, really: its closeness to the Sun, its closeness to the Earth, and if it just happens to be large and active. The best comets meet all three of these requirements, and are truly awesome! Their tails hang over the entire night sky, sometimes the daytime sky too. And in the days before aeroplanes, that was one awesome and scary sight.

We think that comets come into the solar system because passing stars may disturb the Oort Cloud, making some of its comets head towards the Sun. They get pulled towards its huge mass – but why?

You've heard of Albert Einstein, right? He's the guy with wild white hair who rewrote the rules of science early last century. And one of Mr Einstein's genius ideas was this: mass 'bends' space. Yes, that's right! The matter of a body bends the space around it. And the more mass you have in one spot, the more bent that spot gets.

It's basically Einstein's way of describing gravity, all this space-bending business. Imagine space is like the surface of your duvet. At least like your duvet when the bed is made, not crumpled up in a heap, as it normally is first thing in the morning. OK, on this tidy, flat duvet you plonk a planet. Well, not an entire planet, but a simulation of a planet: a football. Better still, a bowling ball, if you have one to hand.

The thing is this: the heavier – or more massive – the ball, the bigger the dip. Not only that, but that dip around the ball seems to pull stuff nearby towards it. If you roll some smaller balls across the bed, you can see exactly what we mean.

Now if you think of your balls as planets and the duvet as the fabric of space, you can see just what Einstein was banging on about. That's how gravity works, because mass bends space!

An experiment you can do without leaving your bed. Great!

Good thinking, mate.

So next time your folks complain about you lazing around, you can tell them you're thinking about Einstein's General Theory of Relativity.

Comets Past and Present

People have always thought that comets were a big deal. The Ancient Chinese used to call comets 'ominous stars' because they believed they brought bad news. And sometimes comets can be very bad news.

Planet Earth's long history is littered with big bangs. The bangs have been impacts from outer space, usually from large comets and asteroids which have managed to break through the atmosphere. The evidence is there in the many craters to be found on our planet's surface. The most famous impact of all was the comet that may have finished off the dinosaurs 65 million years ago.

The bringers of life?

But it's not all bad. Comets contain masses of water. And those comet impacts on Earth in the dim and distant past may have supplied life-giving water to our developing environment. On top of that, it could even be that these comets brought to Earth the kind of chemicals that can create the most basic forms of life. And that means impacts could have played a key part in the development of life, not just on Earth, but also on other planets.

Above: Queen Elizabeth I's courtiers tried to stop her looking up at the great comet of 1577. (She ignored them and looked at it anyway.)

Left: A historical image of a comet.

And how about Comet Swift-Tuttle for drama? The comet is named after the pair who spotted it back in 1862, Lewis Swift and Horace Tuttle. Well done, lads! It comes back into the inner solar system every 133 years or so. In the meantime, we see evidence of it every year. For debris from Comet Swift-Tuttle produces the Perseid meteor shower every August. This incredible sight has been described as looking like stars raining down from heaven.

Does my tail look big in this?

Compared to planets and moons, comets are quite small. But when they come close to the Sun they often produce a gargantuan tail, because of the effect of the Sun's radiation on the comet's body. The tail always points away from the Sun, whichever way the comet is going.

This image combines two photographs of the 3-mile-wide comet Wild-2 – one to show its lumpy surface, and one to show the jets of gas and dust streaming off it. These will form a tail millions of miles long.

Make a Comet Crater!

One of the most famous actual hits on the Earth happened in Arizona, leaving what is now called Meteor Crater. This crater was created about 50,000 years ago, when a rock some 50 metres wide, and weighing 300,000 tons, landed at 30,000 mph.

And you can create this crater in your very own kitchen! Well, kind of...

Steve and Dan prepare for impact

You will need:

- a large bowl or baking pan (do not use glass)
- flour – enough to fill the pan 4cm deep
- some contrasting coloured powder (e.g. cocoa, pepper or turmeric) – enough to lightly cover the flour in a thin layer
- several objects to drop into the flour – e.g. a marble, a small stone, a coin, a grape or other small fruit

How to do it:

1 To keep peace with the grown-ups, cover the floor with newspaper (or even better, do the experiment outside). That will make it much easier to clean up afterwards.
Place the baking pan on the floor or ground and fill it 4cm deep with flour.
Then try to smooth the top of the flour.
Now sieve a thin, contrasting powder on the top (you don't have to cover the lot). If you cover it with the powder, you will need a little more.

2 Pick your first asteroid. Hold the asteroid about waist height and drop it into the flour.

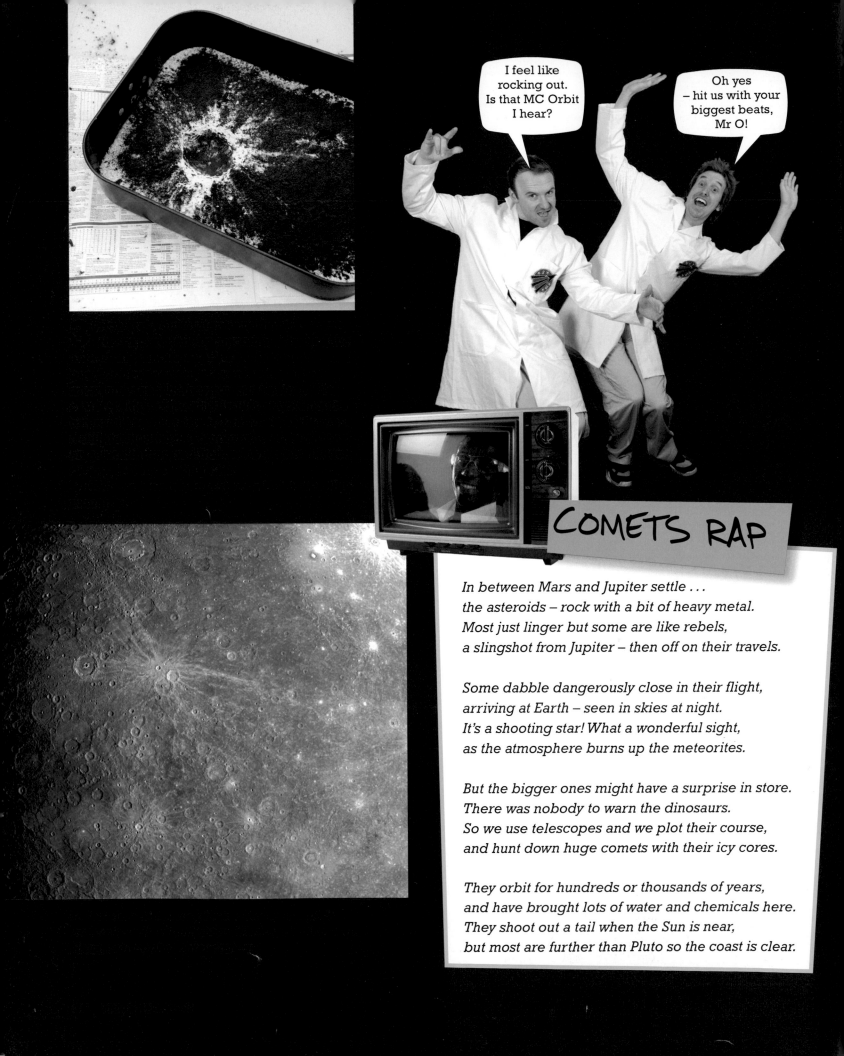

COMETS RAP

In between Mars and Jupiter settle . . .
the asteroids – rock with a bit of heavy metal.
Most just linger but some are like rebels,
a slingshot from Jupiter – then off on their travels.

Some dabble dangerously close in their flight,
arriving at Earth – seen in skies at night.
It's a shooting star! What a wonderful sight,
as the atmosphere burns up the meteorites.

But the bigger ones might have a surprise in store.
There was nobody to warn the dinosaurs.
So we use telescopes and we plot their course,
and hunt down huge comets with their icy cores.

They orbit for hundreds or thousands of years,
and have brought lots of water and chemicals here.
They shoot out a tail when the Sun is near,
but most are further than Pluto so the coast is clear.

TURNED OUT
NASTY
AGAIN

Weather on any planet is controlled by its atmosphere – the layer of gas that surrounds it and which is held in place by the force of gravity. And out there in the solar system that weather can be very different from Earth's, because the atmospheres of other planets are very different from ours.

Welcome to the world of extreme weather – where giant tornadoes spin, toxic rain falls from the sky and massive winds can whip you off your feet. Plenty of possibilities for extreme sports, you might think – but imagine a gale force 555, a wind so mighty as to set loose not just your kite, but also you, your dog and your house!

Things blow hot and cold for Dan and Steve as they try to track down the very wildest weather in the solar system.

What's up, Dan?

I'm thinking about taking off in a high-velocity spacecraft, loaded with tons of fuel, which could **explode** into a billion tiny bits – making it really unlikely that we'd get home again.

Yeah – sounds *exciting*, doesn't it?

And about crash-landing on hostile planets, risking a terrible, lingering death from the heat, the cold, the pressure or the poisonous atmosphere.

Yep. There sure is a lot of wild stuff out there for us to experience!

Wild Spa-cations

The controls are set. Are you ready to embark on the ultimate space cruise? We'll help you choose a wild-weather-chasing space destination for the experience of a lifetime!

● Destination one is planet **Mercury**. The news on its weather is warming. Mercury is the closest planet to the Sun, and at 426°C, hot enough to burn you to a cinder.

Far right: Steve and Dan investigate the art of crash-landing.

● Travellers should know that attempting to land on Mercury comes with only a tiny chance of survival, as the planet moves so fast. It whips round the Sun at almost 30 miles a second! Expert space piloting skills will be needed to touch down in one piece. Bear in mind that Mercury's thin atmosphere will make it almost impossible to slow down as your craft hurtles towards its rocky surface.

If we're going to stand any chance of surviving these journeys we need to start getting in some practice.

● For thrills of the slightly safer kind – if you can spare the one-way journey time of forty years – be wowed by super-chilly **Pluto** and its permanent ice age, a place where the Sun appears a distant star in the always dusky sky.

● An absolute must if you're in the area is a diversion to **Neptune** (that's the blue one below), where the 1,000 mph gales blow freely – perfect for that windsurfing break!

Too right. I'm too pretty to risk my life on a distant planet. How would Earth's girls survive without me?

● If you're working to a budget, how about staying nearer to home? The Red Planet **Mars** boasts tornadoes as high as Mount Everest, covering the whole planet in spectacular dust storms. You'll never get complaints about bringing sand back into your holiday apartment again.

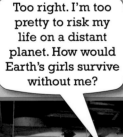

WARNING!

Do be aware that if your vacation becomes a one-way trip, the policy of Space Cadet Tours is not to offer a refund.

Toxic Venus

Venus – the ultimate wild-weather space destination. High winds, extreme surface pressure, a history of volcanoes and blazing heat. Could this be the perfect spot for a couple of space travellers who are looking for a planet (any planet) where they might just survive the landing?

Dan and Steve are hopeful. But they soon discover a few home truths about the Venusian environment.

Venus: hardly your average seaside resort. Those clouds (in the artist's impression above, and photograph, right) are formed of sulphuric acid!

Violent Venus facts

● Its atmosphere is so thick – ninety times thicker than on Earth – that even the strongest telescopes can't see through it.

● It's incredibly hot – any visitor would need a massive amount of protection to prevent themselves being roasted alive.

● Venus has a highly pressurized atmosphere which would crush a human.

● There are thick clouds of sulphuric acid that send down a toxic rain. Before the rain reaches the surface of the planet it evaporates into a deadly poison gas.

● Venus has been shrouded in mystery for decades. At one time, scientists thought of Venus as a kind of sister planet to Earth. It's about the same size – and some even hoped that behind that cloudy veil, it would turn out to be home to some kind of life.

● But it soon became clear that no life could survive there. The unmanned spacecraft that have landed on Venus have either been destroyed on impact or melted in minutes. Dan and Steve must look elsewhere.

I am Space Cadet Steve and I laugh in the face of sulphuric acid rain!

After a soaking with that stuff, you might not have a face left to laugh with…

Dan suffered badly from wind

Wild and Windy Jupiter

If Dan and Steve are into windsurfing, their ideal holiday spot might be **Jupiter**. The winds there are immense. Even though Jupiter is big enough – at 89,000 miles wide – to swallow up all the other planets scrunched together, it still manages a full turn in just under ten hours! A bit blowy then . . .

A quick look at Jupiter through a good telescope will show a planet wrapped in bands of yellow, browns and faint reds. The bands are strips of atmosphere, flowing in different directions. On planet Earth we have two jet streams, narrow air currents that flow in the atmosphere. On Jupiter there are thirty jet streams zipping round the planet!

Dan and Steve are keen – but then discover that there is nowhere to land your spacecraft. Unlike the rocky planets of Earth, Mars and Venus, there is no solid ground on Jupiter to stand on. And if they did manage to get out, they would have to wear special clothing to protect their skin against the deadly effects of ammonia, hydrogen sulphide and ammonium hydrogen – sulphide gases.

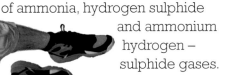

> Massive wind? I can handle that. After years of living with Dan and his baked bean habit, it'll be a breeze!

Above: The black dot on the lower left quarter of Jupiter is the shadow of Io

Below: those storms may be deadly, but they're rather pretty too

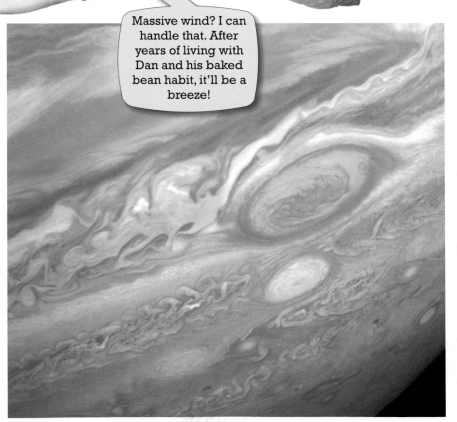

Left: The Great Red Spot is a huge storm that has been raging for at least 400 years on Jupiter. Around its perimeter the winds are moving at more than 200 miles per hour! Unlike hurricanes on Earth, which are low-pressure, the Great Red Spot is high-pressure, so it's more stable – and that's one of the reasons it's lasted so long.

Storm chasers

If you have a smaller budget and can't get to Jupiter, there are plenty of wild and windy places on Earth to keep you busy. Many storm chasers on our own planet follow tornadoes.

A tornado is a violent and dangerous column of air, which can reach wind speeds of more than 300 mph, and stretch more than a mile across. Tornadoes have been spotted on most of the Earth's continents, but the vast majority of them occur in the Tornado Alley region of the United States.

TV weathermen would be out of work in the rest of the solar system. Take Jupiter, for example. It's pretty pointless showing a daily weather chart on 'Jupiter TV' because it would ALWAYS have the Great Red Spot slap bang in the middle of the picture. Same with Saturn – 'Looks like rings in space again today, folks.' And so it is throughout our family of local planets; they've got the weather nailed down. The ice on Europa, the volcanoes on Io, the wind on Jupiter are all permanently wild-weather features.

Now if you want some REAL adventure, come to Earth. Hey, this could be our tourism slogan, should we wish to attract Martians and other aliens to our lovely little planet: 'Come to Earth: You Never Quite Know What Weather You'll Get Next.'

Main: Hurricane Charley in 2004 over Florida, photographed from the International Space Station

Below: Hurricane Isaac, east of Bermuda in 2002

How Windy is It?

Is it breezy, windy or blowing a gale? Here's the table of wind speeds that Sir Francis Beaufort drew up in 1805 and which is still used today. They would have to add quite a few new definitions for Jupiter!

The Beaufort Scale

0	Calm	7	Moderate gale
1	Light air	8	Fresh gale
2	Light breeze	9	Strong gale
3	Gentle breeze	10	Whole gale
4	Moderate breeze	11	Storm
5	Fresh breeze	12	Hurricane
6	Strong breeze		

Eggshell Destruction

Life has never been able to thrive in the harsh conditions on Venus – and its sulphuric acid rain clouds are deadly. To witness the devastating effects of an acidic substance, try this experiment.

You will need:

- eggs – one or more, depending on how many liquids you want to experiment with
- drinking glasses – one for each egg
- vinegar – enough to fill one of your glasses
- a variety of different liquids for experimentation, e.g. cola, orange juice, milk, water

IMPORTANT!
For this experiment, you should only use liquids that are safe to drink.

I predict that this cracking eggs-periment will prove a real break-through, Professor Dan!

Eggs-actly, Professor Steve!

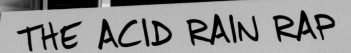

THE ACID RAIN RAP

*On Venus the clouds that cover are sulphuric
with acid that will vanish stuff quicker than magic.
What will corrode and what's fit to withstand it?
Experimentation's needed to help us understand it.*

*An umbrella's no use against this acid rain.
It's made out of nylon which might help explain
why it gives no protection in this type of storm
on a high-pressure planet where weird weather's the norm.*

*Reading your favourite comic or mag
with big blots in the middle could soon become a drag,
while sweets up on Venus start to lose their allure
when the pinks and the purples go brown like manure.*

*Rope can't cope with this acid attack,
sizzling, fuming and then turning black,
and as Granny's best tights turn quickly to mush
this is the type of place you'll wanna leave in a rush.*

Water Milk Orange juice Cola Vinegar

SHORT HOPS, LONG HAULS

It's a key question for any holidaymaker. Should you stay close to home for your hols, or look further afield? (Actually, that's two questions, but you get the drift.)

And so it is with space. Do you stick close to the Earth, take a short hop, catch a few rays, and focus on all that the inner solar system has to offer? Or do you long-haul it to the outer solar system and head for a winter wonderland in space?

These are exactly the kind of questions that face space cadets Dan and Steve as they consider their journey time. Just to reach Mars, in the inner solar system, will take six months, whereas a trip to Saturn will set our travellers back six or seven years. And you can forget about Proxima Centauri, the closest star to the Sun. That would take a space tourist millions of years to reach!

And there's another pressing problem for potential astronauts. Travelling long distances in space is really tough on the body. As Dan and Steve are about to discover . . .

I thought space travel was just sitting around in a rocket with your feet up for months on end.

No, Dan. Space travel is a physically demanding business – so we need to get fit.

What, even fitter than I am already?

Amazingly, even fitter than *that.*

Space Cadet Tours welcomes you aboard today's flight to the Moon and beyond – way beyond!

Far-flung Spa-cations

If you'd prefer a different moon, there are more than 300 others in the solar system. Most are millions of miles away, so please bring something to occupy yourself on the journey. To reach the most exciting moons could take six years.

● All passengers must be in **good shape** because travelling through space in a weightless state can have a few nasty side effects.

● First, you may acquire what is technically known as **'bird legs'**. This is what happens when all the body fluid that's normally pulled down by gravity floats upwards instead – leaving your legs extra-thin like a bird's.

● All that upwards-travelling fluid will also gather in your head, making your face **swollen and puffy**. You may find too that you suffer from a little uncontrolled vomiting while your brain gets used to being weightless.

● All space travellers are recommended to do at least **two hours** of exercise every day, to stop their bones and muscles wasting away. And after months of being weightless in space, walking could be a bit of a problem when you get back to Earth's gravity again.

Dan – are you OK? I don't think you're used to all this exercise.

No – I'm fine, just a bit out of breath, that's all.

You do look *red*.

That, my friend, is what's known as the flush of good health. Quick, give me a hand – I think I'm about to fall over.

Destination Moon

To help them understand the distances involved in space travel, Dan and Steve attempt to recreate the solar system – on a beach. Every metre they run represents a six-million-mile stretch between one of the eight planets and the Sun. They manage to stagger to Mercury, Venus and Mars, but Neptune? No chance. (See page 50 for a chart of actual planetary distances.) Our Space Cadets decide to stick with the Moon – at a more manageable 238,600 miles away from Earth!

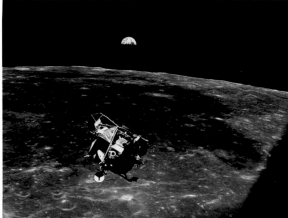

Far left: Edwin 'Buzz' Aldrin sets up an experiment on the Moon, 20 July 1969.

Left: after just 22 hours, the Lunar Module takes off to begin the long journey home to Earth.

Men on the Moon

The first Moon landing forty years ago is one of the great achievements of the human race. The technology was basic. A washing machine today has more computing power than the mission control computer back then. But that makes what was achieved even more amazing.

Four hundred years ago, in the first days of the telescope, Italian astronomer Galileo had seen mountains and valleys on the Moon, and what he thought might be ancient seas. But it was only when we actually visited the Moon that we could really uncover its secrets. Like the fact that it once had volcanoes erupting on its surface.

But what the Apollo missions also found out is that the Moon is geologically dead. It's a four and a half billion-year-old crater-ridden dead rock orbiting the Earth once every 27 days, 7 hours. Nothing much has happened up there for billions of years.

Remember your first words as you took off for the Moon?

Aah . . . I don't recall.

'Help! Help! Let me out. I feel ill.'

Nope, don't remember that at all.

Jack and Luke reckon they made it to the Moon. At least, Jack did.

Destination Other Moons

But as Dan and Steve discover, there are other moons around with more interesting features.

● Strangely shaped moons like **Deimos** ① and **Phobos** ②, which orbit Mars.

● If you fancy bungee jumping, why not consider **Miranda** ③, one of the moons of Uranus? You'll get a very different kind of bungee jump there. Miranda has the highest cliffs in the solar system, at 3 miles high. But Miranda also has very low gravity. That means you'll have a very slow, hovery start to your bungee jump, then pick up bungee speed as you take in the view of the most dramatic cliffs in space!

● A moon which looks like the Death Star from *Star Wars*! **Mimas** ④ circles Saturn and is dominated by a crater over 4 miles deep. This was caused by a collision with a 93-mile-wide comet, almost smashing Mimas up!

● A moon with underwater oceans that could possibly be a home for life. **Europa** ⑤ circles Jupiter and has a wrinkled, fractured surface that suggests it is ice floating on a liquid core.

Our Moving Earth

Another thing for our space travellers to consider is this: our planet Earth is already on a never-ending journey through the solar system. Even though it doesn't feel like it as you go about your day, Earth moves at high speed through space, and is spinning on its axis at the same time. So whatever speed you seem to be moving at, that's never the full story.

Imagine you're travelling in your car down the motorway at 50mph. Even then you are also travelling at 800mph around the Earth's spin axis. Just like all the other planets in the solar system, Earth is constantly spinning.

But there's more. We're not just spinning on the spot. Earth is also travelling in orbit round the Sun. It takes a year to complete the circuit and that's a journey of almost half a billion miles.

It means that, as well as spinning at speed, we are also hurtling through space at 67,000 mph in orbit round the Sun. And on top of all that, the Milky Way Galaxy, which includes our solar system and up to 400 million other stars, is travelling at 1,409,000mph! It's enough to make your head spin. No wonder Dan looks worried!

But why don't we feel the speed at which we're moving? The reason is this. Because the Earth travels so smoothly and because we are moving at exactly the same speed as the Earth beneath our feet, it doesn't feel as if we are on the move at all. We're all being carried along with the ride, like the smoothest lift journey possible, or travelling in a plane but with no bumps or winds or speeding up and slowing down.

The Toilet Paper Solar System

The distances in our solar system are so unbelievably vast that it can be hard to try and imagine them. Stranger still, using a roll of toilet paper can help give us an idea of the very different distances between all our planets in relation to the Sun. Why not give it a whirl?

You will need:

- one roll of toilet paper, with at least 100 sheets
- differently coloured felt-tips or gel pens
- a long hallway, garden or other large space in which to roll out the loo roll

How to do it:

1 Find you long space and put the toilet roll down to the sun of your solar system. Unroll a short section of paper and draw in the first world, specifically you...

2 You will continue to put the sun at the beginning...

I don't understand it. I put a full roll in there yesterday and it's already gone . . .

Steve, I'm not sure if I'm cut out for spending a long time in space.

You might have a point. We may have to accept the truth that you and I are more thinkers than doers.

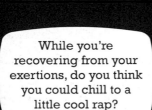

While you're recovering from your exertions, do you think you could chill to a little cool rap?

Bring it on, MC Orbit, my friend!

WILD WEATHER RAP

We're on board a ship going through the space ocean.
That ship is called Earth and it's always in motion.
This is the planet where we started exploration,
but how do we prepare for a further destination?

First to get right is the fitness side,
because a journey to space is no easy ride.
We first walked on the Moon in 1969,
leaving Earth in a rocket – back in eight days' time.

There's no up or down in space so we need some indication,
but luckily we have a map, it uses constellations.
If you know them well you won't get lost on your vacation,
so pack your bags, study hard and choose the right direction.

We're going out to Saturn, where the moons are bizarre.
The biggest one is Titan, whose atmosphere is vast,
but don't forget Mimas, looking like the Death Star!
It's got a four-mile-deep crater as a scar.

WET
AND WILD

'**E**arth' is a funny old name for our home planet, when you think about it. After all, it's mostly water! Almost 71% of the Earth's surface is covered by the oceans, and another 1% is covered by water in lakes and rivers. So only 28% is actually earth. We live on The Water Planet.

All this water makes Earth a quite unique planet in our solar system, one that is home to an amazing variety of life. Life on our planet is thought to have begun in the ocean. And today water makes up 60 – 70% of all living matter, including you!

Water is one of the vital ingredients needed for life, anywhere, to flourish. That's why scientists tend to get very excited if even a mere trace of water is detected on another planet. For the trail of watery wonders in space may well also lead to the discovery of alien life forms!

Dan and Steve are keen to find signs of life on other planets. And they will also need water if they are to survive on their quest – but where will they find it in the dark dry depths of space?

Wee would need to make use of a liquid that **wee** have got a ready supply of. Which would mean that **wee** would never go thirsty.

You don't mean . . . No, that's disgusting. Someone tell me that's not true!

Soggy Spa-cations

Residual water ice in the Vastitas Borealis crater on Mars.

All hot and bothered? Need to cool down? Then your first stop could be our very own Moon. An Indian space probe has just discovered a thin coating of water on some **Moon** dirt. OK, it may not be a tsunami, but it's better than nothing. Especially for Moon-bound Space Cadets!

● Now consider **Mars**, space trekkers. As you have no doubt seen through your telescopes, and as you will see as you fly over the Martian poles, the Red Planet, like our own Water Planet, is blessed with ice caps.

● Mars also has many a riverbed. But don't go thinking about riding the rapids of the Red Planet, folks. The remnants of Mars' mild and moist ancient past have long since dried up.

● Next, water babies, why not hitch a ride on a passing **comet**? In planet Earth's dim and distant past, it may have been these little beauties that brought the water to make our world's oceans.

● But perhaps the most exotic and secretive waterhole of all is **Europa**, one of the 64 moons orbiting Jupiter. If the boffins are right, Europa could be hiding an ocean that contains more water than all the oceans of Earth combined!

The comet Encke orbits the Sun every 3.3 years, following the line of debris it has shed on previous circuits. Earth passes through this trail every October.

The Phoenix Lander has scraped small holes in the surface of Mars, revealing patches of ice.

All this talk of u-rine takes me back to the good old days.

Talk of u-rine *always* gets me thinking about the old days.

Where's There's Water, There's Life

There is one place on Earth that has shown us how important water is for survival – the **Atacama Desert** in Chile, South America. It has one of the most extreme climates on Earth – fifty times drier than the Sahara desert!

And on the Water Planet, that makes the Atacama desert an extraordinary place. You could drive through this desert for hours and see absolutely no sign of life: no plants, no animals, not even bugs in the soil.

Unlike most of our moist little world, it's the dryness that prevents anything living here. It's so dry that even bacteria cannot survive. There is soil in this desert that is more sterile than a hospital operating theatre. In fact, doctors could perform operations out here, if only there was somewhere to plug in the machines that go beep!

This desert has proved that life needs water – so if we're going to find life elsewhere in the solar system, we need to 'follow the water'.

So where shall we start? What about Mars? I could even be the first human to meet a Martian. Imagine the fame, the glory…

But, Steve, didn't they say that the water on Mars disappeared years ago?

Hmmm, you might be right. I think it's time to consult my trusty Cadet's Guide!

The high altitude and the clear skies of the Atacama Desert make it one of the best places on Earth to view the night sky. It's also home to the most powerful telescope in the world, one that can see into deepest space.

Is There Life on Mars?

We know more about Mars – the fourth planet out from the Sun – than anywhere else in the solar system (other than our own planet Earth, of course).

For one thing, it's the closest planet surface that we can see through our telescopes. Venus is shrouded in a veil of mysterious cloud, but Mars is there for all to see. Like Earth, Mars has a 24-hour day, it has seasons, and it has polar caps. For many years, some astronomers also thought it had canals, made by parched Martians. But that turned out to be a rather barmy idea.

Today, the probes that orbit Mars and the robotic rovers on its surface have sent back images that seem to show that water once flowed freely on the Red Planet's surface.

Features like this massive canyon – the Valles Marineris – may have been created by water in the same way as happens on Earth.

One of the most amazing sights that our planet has to offer is the Grand Canyon in Arizona, USA . It's astonishing that something as massive as this canyon was made by running water wearing away the rock over millions of years. But compared with what we've found on Mars, the Grand Canyon is not that grand at all. To match Mars' Valles Marineris in size, it would have to be three times deeper and stretch all the way across America!

So what happened to the flowing water on Mars that created the monster canyon? Its disappearance is all down to the thinness of its atmosphere – the layer of gas surrounding the planet.

Valles Marineris

Below left: the Tharsis volcanoes are covered in pale blue clouds of ice to the left; the Marineris canyon system is on the right.

We still have plenty of water on Earth because our atmosphere is thick enough to keep in enough of the Sun's warmth so that the oceans don't freeze. Mars' atmosphere is very thin – too thin to keep in the heat. So Mars got colder and colder until its liquid water disappeared.

Any water left there – and we've not found very much yet – is now locked away as ice either in its polar ice caps or below the surface. Meanwhile we are still searching for signs of life on Mars. So keep listening to those news reports…

I'm out there somewhere . . .

Europa – the Enigma

Europa is a beautiful, but tortured, ice world. The Cassini spacecraft took six years of travelling to get close enough to send these detailed pictures back. And the more we have seen of it, the odder it looks, with its strange fractured surface. It appears twisted and cracked, almost as if it's disconnected from the rest of it – or as if its loose skin is from spinning at a different rate to the rest of Europa.

Europa's unusual textured surface has been compared to a ball of string. It looks as if it has broken up and 'floated' into new positions. The darker lines in these colour-enhanced images (below and right) are ridges and fractures, which can run for thousands of miles.

Everything about Europa suggests its icy surface is floating on water. We haven't touched it, we haven't even seen it, but this tiny moon of the Jupiter system could be the key to finding life beyond Earth.

The big question about the underwater oceans we think are lurking beneath Europa's surface is whether life could start deep under the watery surface, away from the energy provided by the heat and light from the Sun's rays.

On Earth we've found forms of life that do just that. Deep in a mine in South Africa are tiny microbes, which gain their energy not from the Sun but from the chemical uranium.

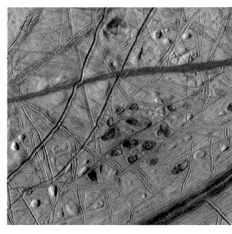

So we know it is possible for life to survive deep beneath a planet's surface. The big problem with Europa is that it is so far away and its icy surface is so thick, exploring what's underneath is going to be incredibly difficult. But that makes it even more tantalizing. Have we found somewhere in our solar system where life exists?

A moon with oceans under the surface that could contain some kind of extra-terrestrial life! That's amazing.

Yes, indeed. It would be amazing to see those underwater oceans for ourselves – but it doesn't sound like that's going to be possible for a long, long time.

Aww, what a shame.

In the meantime, I suggest we perform a highly scientific experiment in order to experience how it would really feel to be immersed in Europa's oceans. Here goes!

Dirty Water Clean-Up

Dan is more than a little shocked to find out what he'll have to drink in space – his own wee! Luckily, space urine has to go undergo a thorough water purification treatment which makes it into clean, drinkable water. You can try a similar experiment at home (though remember – this definitely does NOT work for wee!).

You will need:

- a hot sunny day – this won't work otherwise
- a large clear bowl
- clingfilm
- a drinking glass
- 2-3 teaspoons of salt
- a few drops of food colouring
- water
- a pebble

> Ooh Steve, you know I can't stop thinking about the drinking 'problem' up there in space.

> Don't worry yourself, Dan. Astronauts use a special whizzy machine that purifies the wee and turns it into nice clean water.

> But that doesn't solve our immediate problem – how to find the loo on a space ship!

3 Cover the bowl loosely with the clingfilm. Now place the pebble in the middle of the clingfilm directly above the top of the glass – this is very important. The clingfilm should be loose enough so that the pebble dips down into the glass.

4 [illegible] How did this happen?

The Sun's energy made it very hot inside the bowl. This caused the water in the disgusting solution to evaporate and rise up to the underside of the clingfilm, where it condensed [illegible]

THE WEE TO WATER RAP

Up in a space ship there's no room to take water
so you need to drink something that seriously oughta
taste terrible. Wee is the space drink of choice.
And to show how that's done we need samples from the boys.

Next step in the quest for safe wee drinking surety
is mixing in charcoal, which gets rid of impurities.
In space, when you're weightless, the method's to spin it,
to isolate the nasty organic matter in it.
On Earth this energy source does the same,
as next in the process, it's time for a flame.

Boiling the urine makes it soon disappear
as the liquid evaporates, then re-liquefies here.
The brine has been boiled off. The brew is refined,
so leaving a liquid that's purer behind.

One final filtration should complete the quest
so step forward, cadets, here's a drink on request.
Now that the nasty stuff's all been dispersed
it still smells pretty bad, but it quenches that thirst.

Space Cadet Quiz

1 The hottest body in our solar system is:

  a. Dan sunbathing on a beach

  b. Our star, the Sun

  c. The planet Mercury

2 If you were to travel to the moon Io, you would have a very weird experience. What would it be?

  a. You would constantly fall over, slipping around on its icy surface (like Dan on a pair of skates)

  b. You might find your house in a different place to where you left it, due to the movement of Io's surface

  c. You would have enough pizza to eat for millions of years

3 The icy rings of Saturn were first spotted by grumpy Italian astronomer Galileo. He thought the rings were:

  a. Giant hoops

  b. Dirty marks on his telescope

  c. Ears

4 When visiting Erta Ale volcano in Ethiopia, you'll notice a terrible smell. The massive stink is created by:

  a. Sulphur

  b. Dan's bottom

  c. Very high winds

5 Close up, a comet's tail is a similar consistency to:

  a. Smoke

  b. Pizza

  c. Mashed potato

Hey, hopeful Space Hoppers! Just to see if you were listening, we've devised a totally out-of-this world quiz.

Give it a go and see if you know enough to be a Space Cadet of the future. Seven correct answers and you can definitely join our crew – you'll know more than we do!

6 'Earth' is a funny old name for our home planet, as 71% of its surface is covered by:

a. Trees

b. Custard

c. Water

7 On the moon Miranda, gravity is so low that you can bungee off its 12-mile-high cliffs without a bungee! But Miranda is a moon of which planet?

a. Jupiter

b. Saturn

c. Uranus

8 One of the moons of Saturn, Mimas, has got such an enormous crater that it's been compared to:

a. The Death Star from *Star Wars*

b. The biggest zit in the universe

c. The Grand Canyon

9 At 460°C, the surface temperature of planet Venus is hot enough to melt:

a. Venus

b. Lead

c. Chocolate

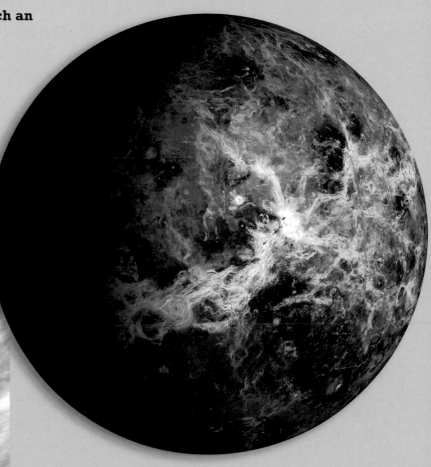

10 The Great Red Spot on Jupiter is thought to be:

a. A massive erupting volcano

b. Jam

c. A storm that's been raging for at least 400 years

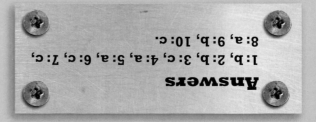

Answers

1:b, 2:b, 3:c, 4:a, 5:a, 6:c, 7:c, 8:a, 9:b, 10:c.

Glossary

Aliens

Extraterrestrial life that comes from beyond planet Earth. Alien life could possibly exist in any shape or form, perhaps microscopic bugs smaller than a pinhead, or maybe a much larger species of creature. No one knows, because alien life has not yet been found.

Asteroid

Small bodies, composed of rock and metal, in orbit around the Sun. The main asteroid belt sits between the orbits of Mars and Jupiter.

Atmosphere

A layer of gases that may surround a body, if it has enough mass. This normally means planets, but some moons are big enough to have atmospheres.

Carbon footprint

A measure of the damage done to the environment by the behaviour of a person, object or organization.

Comet

Small bodies in orbit about the Sun. When they come close enough to the Sun, comets have fuzzy 'atmospheres' and sometimes a tail. Comets are loose collections of ice, dust and rock.

Constellation

An area of the sky in which the brighter visible stars seem to form a pattern. The stars in a constellation just happen to appear close together in the sky when viewed from Earth, but in reality they lie many millions of miles apart in space. Famous constellations include Orion and Ursa Major (the Great Bear).

Crater

A circular dent made in the surface of a moon or planet by the high-speed impact of a much smaller body (usually a comet or an asteroid).

Earthquake

A sudden release of energy in the Earth's crust that creates tremors and can often cause cracks in the earth.

Extraterrestrial

Extraterrestrial means any object or being beyond (extra-) the planet Earth (-terrestrial). The term E.T. is often used to mean 'alien'.

Galaxy

A massive population of stars that is held together by gravity. A galaxy will also contain a lot of gas and dust between the stars. Galaxies can range from dwarfs which may have only 10 million stars to giants with one trillion (or million million) stars. Our Sun is one of the billions of stars in our own Milky Way Galaxy. Other famous galaxies include Andromeda and the Magellanic Clouds.

Gravity

A natural action by which bodies with mass attract one another. Gravity is responsible for keeping the Earth in orbit round the Sun and the Moon in orbit about the Earth. It is also responsible for tides, which can affect the oceans of Earth as well as the solid rock on moons like Io.

Meteor

The visible streak of light that is seen in the sky when a solid object enters the atmosphere of the Earth.

Milky Way

The Milky Way is our Galaxy, where our solar system is located. It is one of billions of galaxies in the Universe.

Orbit

An orbit is the curved path of one body around another, like the orbit of a planet round the Sun. The natural phenomenon that keeps bodies in orbit is gravity.

Planet

A body orbiting a star. The body is big enough to be rounded by its own gravity, but not so big that it burns like a star. Planets can be rocky, like Earth, Venus and Mars, or gas giants, like Jupiter and Saturn. There are also **dwarf planets**, such as Pluto.

Probe

A space probe is a space exploration mission where a robot spacecraft leaves the Earth and goes into space to visit the Moon, other planets or deep space.

Rocket

A vehicle which uses a jet of fast-moving fluid from an engine to obtain thrust. Some rockets are spacecraft, which travel into space by escaping the gravity of Earth.

Rover

A space exploration vehicle made to move across the surface of other planets and moons.

Solar system

The population of objects which includes the Sun and the eight planets bound to it by gravity, including: the four small inner planets, Mercury, Venus, Earth and Mars (which are mostly made of rock and metal); the four outer planets, Jupiter, Saturn, Uranus and Neptune (which are mostly made of hydrogen and helium); and all the minor bodies, such as asteroids, comets and dwarf planets, like Pluto. (Note: Until a few years ago, Pluto was regarded as part of our solar system – one of nine planets.)

Space

Tricky. Let's call it the limitless, 3-D extent in which objects and events occur in the Universe. Within space, objects have position and direction.

Star

A massive, luminous ball of gas that is held together by gravity. The star in our solar system is the Sun. Other stars are visible in the night sky, when they are not outshone by the Sun. Humans group stars into constellations to make stargazing easier.

Stratosphere

The second major layer of Earth's atmosphere, just above the troposphere and below the mesosphere.

Telescope

A device for looking at faraway objects. Telescopes use lenses or mirrors to make distant things appear far closer.

Volcano

An opening in a planet's surface or crust which allows hot magma, ash and gases to escape from below the surface.

Picture credits

Happy space hopping, Earthlings!

Knitting for Children

Knitting for Children

35 SIMPLE KNITS KIDS WILL LOVE TO MAKE

Claire Montgomerie

CICO BOOKS
LONDON NEW YORK

Published in 2010 by CICO Books

An imprint of Ryland Peters & Small Ltd

20–21 Jockey's Fields

519 Broadway, 5th Floor

London WC1R 4BW

New York, NY 10012

www.cicobooks.com

10 9 8 7 6 5 4 3 2 1

A CIP catalog record for this book is
available from the Library of Congress and
the British Library.

ISBN-13: 978 1 907030 64 2

Printed in China

Editor: Kate Haxell
Designer: Elizabeth Healey
Photographers: Terry Benson, Martin Norris,
    and Ian Boddy
Stylists: Emma Hardy and Rose Hammick

Contents

Introduction

There are many reasons to learn to knit, especially as a child. The craft of knitting is not only a fun pastime, it can also be beneficial to children's development. Knitting involves a lot of counting and simple math, as well as being a relaxing and therapeutic occupation, which means that it can aid learning and concentration in some children, especially in those with learning difficulties or attention disorders.

However, knitting books aimed specifically at children are hard to find and one thing that I have discovered through running kids' knitting workshops is that teaching a child to knit is very different from teaching an adult. I have often found that adult-specific knitting books are too complicated or boring for youngsters, yet ones aimed at children are just too simple or babyish, which can discourage them from taking up the craft. Although teaching kids is different from teaching adults, children can most definitely cope with quite challenging patterns, in fact this will help to hold their interest. My experiences have led me to aim to write an interesting, informative, and fun book, aimed solely at children, with lots of alluringly colorful patterns to hold their interest.

I believe that anyone can learn to knit; all it takes is practice and perseverance, but not all children want to commit themselves. However, many of the projects in this book are so small and simple that I hope they will be keen to move onto the next one, and will not even realize that they are progressing through the techniques. Patterns have different skill levels and use the techniques the child will be learning in an interesting yet repetitive way, so they do not know that they are effectively "swatching"—as an adult would do—while they learn.

I have chosen yarns that are easy to use and often formulated especially for children, utilizing a mix of natural fibers to ensure they are kind to young, sensitive skin and man-made fibers to make them durable and easy to wash and care for. However, I have also suggested alternatives so you and your child can play with the look of the projects and use remnants or yarns that are to hand, as many of the patterns use very small amounts of yarn.

Before you dive into the patterns, please do take the time to read my tips on teaching your child to knit (pages 8–11), as I hope my hints and tricks will help make the experience enjoyable and ensure the memory is a warm and happy one for all involved. Most important of all, don't forget to have fun!

Claire Montgomerie

Teaching kids to knit

Through teaching knitting workshops for children, I have developed a few priceless and failsafe practices that should ensure knitting will become a fun hobby for any child. Even if you do not follow them all rigidly, I recommend you stick at least to the simple tools and materials and have a play with the techniques and tips to find out what your child enjoys to knit.

Many people ask me what is the ideal age to teach a child to knit. The truthful answer is "how long is a piece of string?" It really does depend on the child. It is possible for some children to learn the very basics as young as four or five, but this is rare. I have found that the best age is seven or eight, as by this age most children have fully developed motor skills and hand–eye coordination, and can concentrate for longer periods of time. They will also be more likely to take all the techniques in and adopt knitting as a hobby and skill that they will never lose.

Another common question is about which tools to choose. Most people instinctively reach for the larger needles when teaching children, but even for adults large needles can be unwieldy and uncomfortable to use, while children's hands are just too small to cope. Choose size US 6–10 (4–6mm) needles, of a length that it manageable—7½–10in (18–25cm) long is great. You can find needles especially for children that are extra-short with smiley face or patterned decorations, or made from brightly colored plastic, all of which should make them instantly desirable to the young eye.

Choose smooth and stretchy yarn such as wool or acrylic, or a mixture of either of these with other fibers. Don't try fancy yarns at the start, as they may be forgiving when it comes to hiding mistakes, but they may also cause errors through snagging and lack of definition in the stitches.

It is very helpful to cast on for a child and knit a few rows before showing them how to do it themselves, as it is much easier for them to work into a row than a cast-on edge. It also helps them feel as if they have got going already and won't cause them to become discouraged by the sometimes difficult-to-master cast-on technique. A perfect number to cast on is 20 stitches, enough to be substantial and yet not so many that a child will be overwhelmed by each row. It is an easy-to-remember, easy-to-count number that will make it simple to tell if the child has gained or lost stitches and help them to spot their mistakes. If they are having some difficulties with their counting, this will help them with those at the same time.

Go slowly with your child at first, they are generally happy just playing with the yarn and techniques—make the learning like a game. Try to vary the activity as you teach, so have pompom makers and French knitters to hand to embellish the knitting and break up the monotony of knit stitch, especially when you notice any concentration lapses. Don't make them knit for too long. It is a repetitive skill that can cause an ache in the hands of an unpracticed knitter. Short, fun lessons with breaks in between will prevent children from feeling that they are being forced to knit and will make them look forward to picking up the knitting again. You do not have to knit every day, so long as you knit regularly. Perhaps you can find time to knit during a favorite cartoon or before bedtime to unwind. Maybe Saturday evenings will be knitting time. Any quality time with mom, dad or grandma will be eagerly anticipated and if you include all your children in some way, or even their friends, they will want to do it more as it will feel more like a group activity and will be something they can share and talk about.

Have patience with your child; it seems patronising to say so, but sometimes, after a long day together, a parent can be less patient with his or her own child, especially if they really want them to share in the love of

something dear to them. Even if a child's work is a terrible mess, never rip it back as this can undermine their confidence in their ability. Let them see their progression from wonky, and perhaps holey, to beautiful, even knitting. Children often end up with little upside down triangles of knitting, which are caused by increasing many stitches through making unplanned holes and messing up the first stitch of the row. If this happens, don't rip back, but show them how to decrease some stitches by knitting two together so they don't end up getting bored by knitting across a really long row.

Finally, the best tip I can give you is to make it fun! While an adult will happily spend hours knitting swatches that will eventually go either into the bin or a reference file, children want to know what they are making and see the results quite quickly or they may lose interest. Therefore, small projects such as a change purse or mp3 cover are preferable to that standard adult beginner project, the scarf. If it has to be a scarf, make it a mini version for their teddy or doll: perhaps you can make a similar one for your child at the same time so they can dress their toys to match their own outfit and so that you can knit something together.

Knitting should always be relaxing and fun, otherwise, what's the point? So just ensure you both enjoy the process and do not put too much emphasis on perfectly finished knitting. Be flexible and encourage your child to use their imagination; projects can evolve as they are knitted, developing into a final piece that is dictated by the shape of the fabric. Every child is unique and they have a very different view of the world to adults, so let them form fabulous creations from their fabrics, and perhaps, in return, they can also teach you a thing or two about knitting!

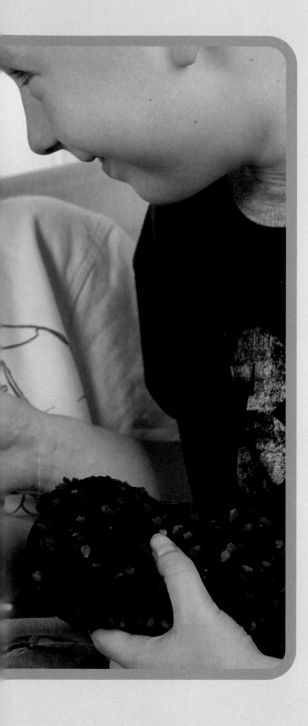

Techniques

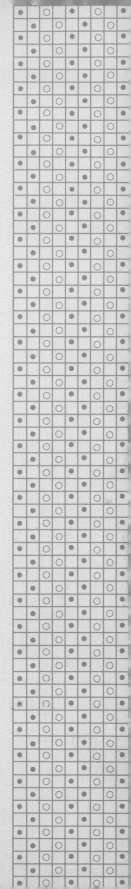

Tools

To start with all you need are knitting needles and some yarn, but there are other things you might want to get as you do more knitting.

▽ Knitting needles come in different materials and colors. The color makes no difference, but the material does. Try using bamboo needles at first, because the yarn tends to slip around less on these.

△ There are lots and lots of different colors and types of yarn to choose from.

▽ Stitch holders are used when you need to set some stitches aside to come back to later.

△ Point protectors slip onto the tips of the needles when you are not knitting and stop your stitches falling off. They also stop the needles making holes in your knitting bag.

▷ Some yarns are very strong, you'll need scissors to cut them.

▷ Thick pins are best for holding bits of knitting together when you sew them up.

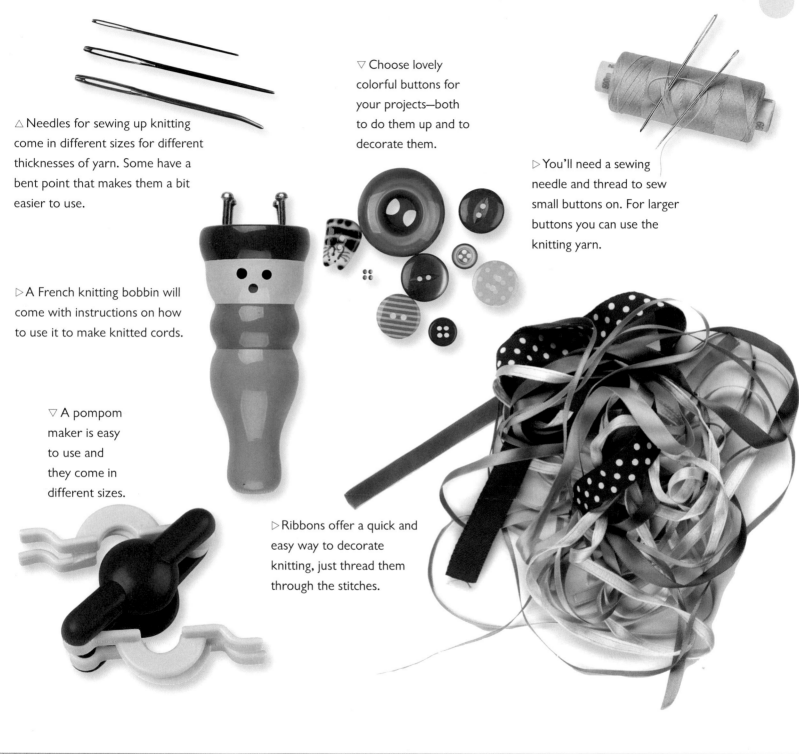

△ Needles for sewing up knitting come in different sizes for different thicknesses of yarn. Some have a bent point that makes them a bit easier to use.

▷ A French knitting bobbin will come with instructions on how to use it to make knitted cords.

▽ A pompom maker is easy to use and they come in different sizes.

▽ Choose lovely colorful buttons for your projects—both to do them up and to decorate them.

▷ You'll need a sewing needle and thread to sew small buttons on. For larger buttons you can use the knitting yarn.

▷ Ribbons offer a quick and easy way to decorate knitting, just thread them through the stitches.

Holding the yarn and needles

There is no one correct way to hold the yarn and needles, everyone finds their own comfortable position, but if you follow my suggestions, you will find it easier to keep an even gauge (tension) when knitting.

There are two most common ways of holding the needles: like a pen or like a knife.

You can hold each needle in the same way, or have each hand use a different way.

Remember that even if you are left-handed you can knit like this, as both hands do some work. However, "lefties" may find continental style easier because the yarn is held in the left hand.

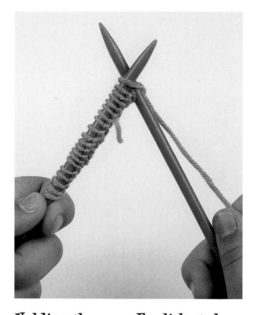

Holding the yarn English style

In English-style knitting, the yarn is held in the right hand.

The ball end of the yarn is wrapped around the right-hand little finger in order to control the amount and speed of yarn feeding through from the ball, and so to control the gauge (tension) of the work (see page 23). The yarn then passes under the two middle fingers and over the pointing finger, which helps to "flick" the yarn around the needle as you knit. If this is too hard at first, you can simply grip the yarn with the right hand and "throw" it round the needle.

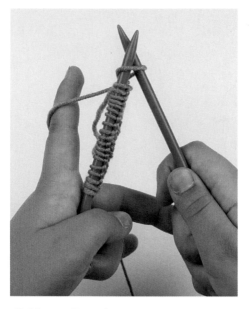

Holding the yarn continental style

Wrap the yarn around the little or middle finger of the left hand, then pass it over the pointing finger of the same hand to hold the yarn taut. Some people like to wrap the yarn just around their pointing finger a few times, but this can cause a tight knitting gauge (tension).

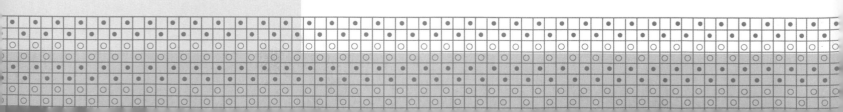

Slip knot and cast on

There are many ways to cast on, but for beginners this is the simplest way, so use this to start with—you can progress to something harder once you have mastered knitting. The first step is to make a slip knot, which will also be your first stitch.

When you are knitting, the yarn leading to the ball is called the "ball-end" of the yarn.

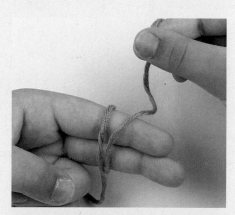

1 Front to back, wind the yarn around two fingers twice to make two loops.

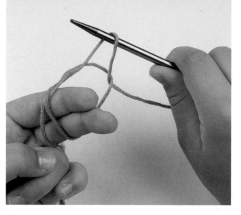

2 Slip a kitting needle under the first loop and hook the second loop through the first one using the tip of the needle.

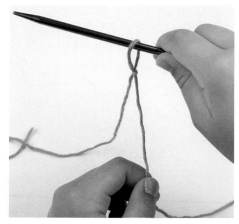

3 Pull on the ends of the yarn to make the slip knot tight on the needle.

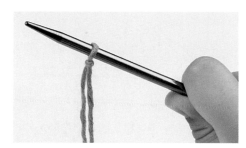

4 You have made your first stitch.

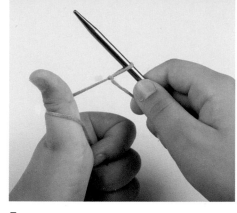

5 Holding the needle in your right hand, make a loop around your left thumb with the ball-end of the yarn.

6 Slip the needle under the loop.

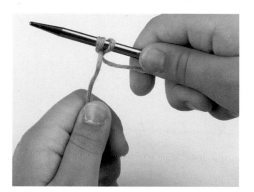

7 Remove your thumb and pull the stitch tight on the needle.

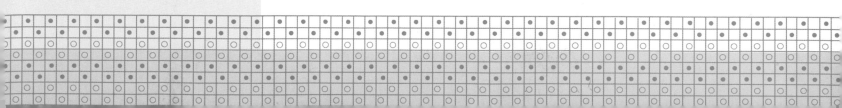

Knit stitch

There are only two stitches in knitting, knit stitch and purl stitch: so there isn't very much to learn!

The knit stitch is the simplest of all stitches. To practice, cast on some stitches and then you can knit every row until you feel you have learned the basic technique.

Knitting every row forms the ridged fabric called garter stitch, which is the simplest stitch pattern (see page 24).

Stockinette (stocking) stitch pattern is made by working one row of knit stitch and one row of purl stitch (see page 20) alternately throughout the fabric.

The aim is to hold the needle with the stitches on in your left hand and the empty needle in your right hand, and to transfer all stitches onto the right-hand needle by knitting a row.

English style

1 Insert the tip of the right-hand needle into the next stitch on the left-hand needle, from the left side of the stitch so that you are going from the front to the back of the knitting.

2 Holding the ball-end of the yarn at the back of the knitting, wrap this yarn around the right-hand needle with your right hand, passing the yarn underneath then over the point of the right-hand needle.

3 Bring a loop of yarn through the stitch on the left-hand needle.

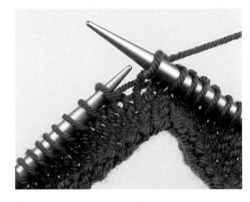

4 Slip the loop off the left-hand needle to complete the stitch, which is now on your right-hand needle.

Repeat these steps with each stitch, until all the stitches on the left-hand needle have been transferred to the right-hand needle. This completes the row. To start a new row, swap the needles in your hands so that the stitches are in your left hand and the yarn is in position at the start of the row.

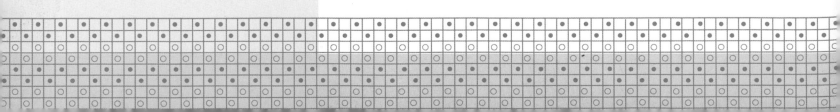

Continental style

1 Insert the tip of the right-hand needle into the next stitch on the left-hand needle, from the left side of the stitch so that you are going from the front to the back of the knitting.

2 Holding the ball-end of the yarn at the back with your left hand, pick this end of the yarn with your right-hand needle.

3 Bring the loop of yarn through the stitch on the left-hand needle.

4 Slip the loop off the left-hand needle to complete the stitch, which is now on your right-hand needle.

 Repeat these steps with each stitch, until all the stitches on the left-hand needle have been transferred to the right-hand needle. This completes the row. To start a new row, swap the needles in your hands so that the stitches are in your left hand and the yarn is in position at the start of the row.

Purl stitch

Most of purl stitch is the other way around to knit stitch. You still hold the needle with stitches on in your left hand, but you insert the right-hand needle a different way into each stitch and you hold the yarn at the front. Work every other row in purl to create stockinette (stocking) stitch (see page 24).

English style

1 Insert the tip of the right-hand needle into the next stitch on the left-hand needle, from the right side of the stitch so that you are going from the back to the front of the knitting.

2 Holding the ball-end of the yarn at the front of the knitting, wrap this yarn around the right-hand needle with your right hand, passing the yarn over and around the right-hand needle.

3 Bring the loop of yarn through the stitch on the left-hand needle.

4 Slip the loop off the left-hand needle to complete the stitch, which is now on your right-hand needle.

Repeat these steps with each stitch, until all the stitches on the left-hand needle have been transferred to the right-hand needle. This completes the row. To start a new row, swap the needles in your hands, so that the yarn is in position at the start of the row, and begin a knit row to make stockinette (stocking) stitch.

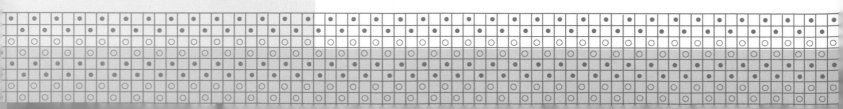

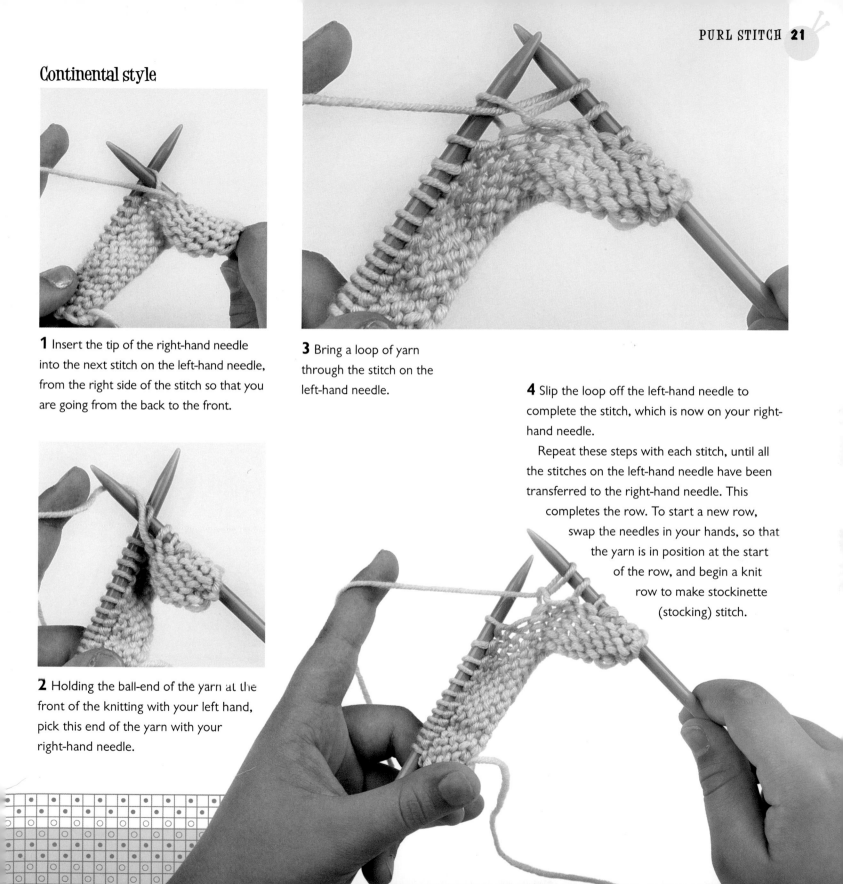

Continental style

1 Insert the tip of the right-hand needle into the next stitch on the left-hand needle, from the right side of the stitch so that you are going from the back to the front.

2 Holding the ball-end of the yarn at the front of the knitting with your left hand, pick this end of the yarn with your right-hand needle.

3 Bring a loop of yarn through the stitch on the left-hand needle.

4 Slip the loop off the left-hand needle to complete the stitch, which is now on your right-hand needle.

Repeat these steps with each stitch, until all the stitches on the left-hand needle have been transferred to the right-hand needle. This completes the row. To start a new row, swap the needles in your hands, so that the yarn is in position at the start of the row, and begin a knit row to make stockinette (stocking) stitch.

Bind (cast) off

When you have finished knitting you need to bind (cast) off so that all your work doesn't just unravel!

1 First knit two stitches (see page 18).

2 Slip the tip of your left-hand needle into the first stitch you knitted and lift it over the stitch closest to the tip of the needle.

3 Lift the first stitch over the second one and drop it off both needles.

4 Knit one more stitch, so there are two on the right-hand needle again, and repeat all the steps until all you have left is one stitch on the right-hand needle. All the other stitches have been bound (cast) off.

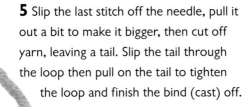

5 Slip the last stitch off the needle, pull it out a bit to make it bigger, then cut off yarn, leaving a tail. Slip the tail through the loop then pull on the tail to tighten the loop and finish the bind (cast) off.

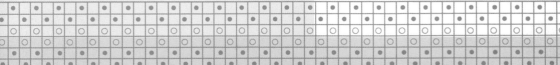

Gauge (tension)

Everybody tends to knit at a different gauge (tension), which means how big or small your stitches are, or how loosely or tightly you knit.

Gauge (tension) varies from knitter to knitter and also when different stitch patterns, yarn fibers, and needle materials are used. The two swatches below have the same number of stitches and rows and were knitted in the same yarn with the same needles, but they were made by two different people. One person has a much looser gauge (tension) than the other, so their swatch is bigger.

A gauge (tension) swatch is used to make sure that you are knitting at the gauge (tension) called for in the pattern. This is essential because the projects are designed to fit certain sizes, so if your gauge (tension) is too loose your project will be too big, and if it is too tight, the project will be too small.

To make a gauge (tension) swatch you need to knit a small square about 4 x 4in (10 x 10cm) in the main yarn and stitch

used in the pattern. Lay the swatch flat, place a ruler on it, and count the number of stitches per inch (centimeter).

If you find you have more stitches per inch (centimeter) than asked for in the pattern, then your gauge (tension) is too tight and you need to make it looser. The best way to do this is to increase the size of knitting needle you use until the gauge (tension) is as close as you can get it. If there are fewer stitches than required, then your gauge (tension) is too loose, and you need to decrease the size of knitting needle you use.

Of course, knitting a gauge (tension) swatch takes time and with some small projects where a good fit is not needed, such as some accessories and toys, you do not need to knit a swatch.

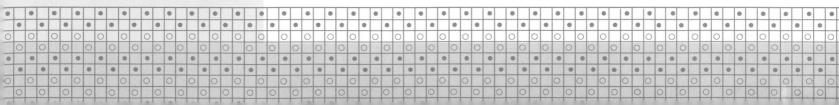

Stitch patterns

Depending on how you combine knit and purl stitches, you can make various stitch patterns to produce knitted fabrics that feel and look very different. These are the four stitch patterns you will find in this book.

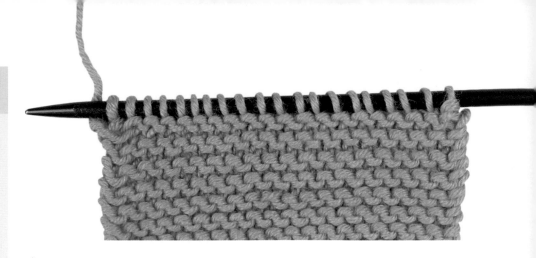

Garter stitch

Knitting every row forms a ridged fabric called garter stitch, which is the simplest stitch pattern. It is the same on both sides and so is a flat, even fabric that is perfect for scarves or edges.

Stockinette (stocking) stitch

This is made by alternately working one row of knit stitch and one row of purl stitch. This makes a fabric that is different on each side. The knit, or plain, side is flat and the stitches look like little "V"s (above left). The purl side is bumpy and textured, with the stitches like little wiggles (above right), and is called reverse stockinette (stocking) stitch.

This fabric curls slightly and so is best used in projects that need to be sewn up, which flattens the curly edges.

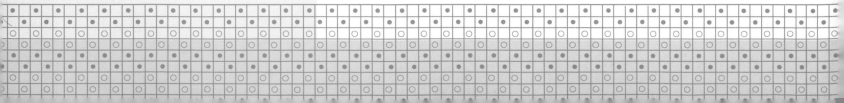

Seed (moss) stitch

Seed (moss) stitch is made by working alternate knit and purl stitches across the same row. As you hold the yarn at the back for knit stitches and at the front for purl stitches, you need to move it after each stitch.

After a knit stitch you must pass the yarn in between the needles to the front of the knitting to work the next purl stitch. After a purl stitch you must pass the yarn in between the needles to the back to make the next knit stitch.

In each row you knit the stitches that were knitted in the last row, and purl those that were purled to create the bumpy texture.

Rib stitch

Rib stitch is created like seed (moss) stitch by working knits and purls alternately across a row. But in each row you knit the stitches that were purled in the last row and vice versa to make the vertical stripes of stitches.

Shaping

To shape a knitted piece you have to increase or decrease the number of stitches on the needles. Here are the simplest ways.

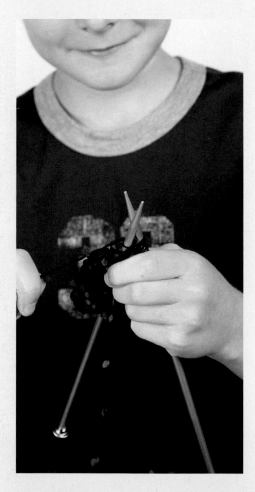

Increasing (inc1)

1 Knit into the front of the next stitch on the left-hand knitting needle, but do not slip it off the needle.

2 With the stitch still on the left-hand needle and the yarn at the back, knit into the back of the same stitch and then slip it off the needle.

3 You have made one stitch into two stitches and so increased by one.

Decreasing (k2tog)

1 Insert the right-hand needle through the fronts of the second then the first stitches on the left-hand needle, from left to right.

2 Then knit the two stitches together, knitting in the usual way (see page 18), and slide both from the left-hand needle.

3 You have made two stitches into one stitch and so decreased by one.

Yarnover (yo)

Wrapping the yarn over the needle creates a small hole in the work and an extra stitch. If you only want the hole and not an increase, you must knit two together to decrease (see opposite) straight after the yo.

1 Bring the yarn forward between the needles, then take it over the right-hand needle and hold it at the back.

2 Knit the next stitch. Work in pattern to the end of the row.

3 On the next row, purl into the loop of the yo as if it were a normal stitch and continue in pattern to the end of the row.

4 Where you made the yo, a small hole is formed, perfect for threading a ribbon through or as a little buttonhole.

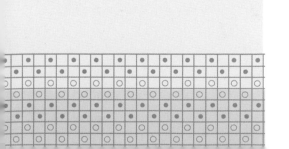

Changing color

When you want to make striped fabrics, or you run out of a ball of yarn, you need to add a new ball at the beginning of the row.

1 Tie the new yarn around the tail of the old yarn, keeping the knot loose.

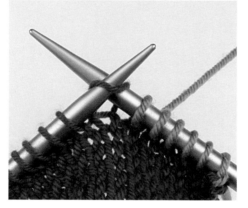

2 Push the knot up next to stitches the pull it tight. Work the next row using the new yarn.

Picking up stitches

Sometimes you need to work a neat edge along the side of a fabric you have already knitted, which is why you need to know how to make the first line of stitches for this edge: this is called picking up stitches. Always do this with the right side of the fabric facing you and try to space the stitches you pick up at equal intervals.

1 Hold the needle in your right hand and insert it through the fabric from front to back where you want to pick up the stitch.

2 Wrap a new piece of yarn around the needle, as if to knit a stitch.

3 Pull the loop through the knitted fabric to the front. Continue in this way along the edge until all the stitches are picked up. Work on these stitches as instructed in the pattern.

Sewing up

Sewing up knitting can be done in many ways, but using a whip stitch is the easiest. However, you can see the stitches quite easily so sometimes it is nice to make a feature of this by using a different color yarn to the one used in the project.

1 Secure the yarn to one piece of fabric with a few little stitches on the back. Lay the pieces to be joined next to each other, right sides up. Insert the needle into the front of one piece of fabric, then up from the back of the adjoining fabric.

2 Repeat along the seam.

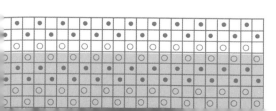

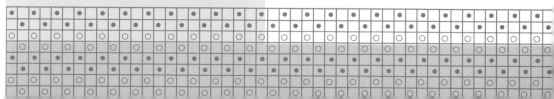

Pompoms

Pompoms are so simple to make. You can make them from rings of cardboard, but buying a plastic pompom maker is so much quicker and simpler, and you don't have to make a new one each time you want to make pompoms. You can buy makers in all shapes and sizes—even heart shaped!

Some types work a little differently to the one shown, so always read the instructions on the pack before you start.

Here is a little tip: try cutting the end of the yarn for tying before you begin so that you don't have to put down the pompom maker in the middle of cutting the pompom.

1 Wind yarn around each half of the pompom maker.

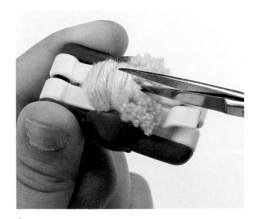

2 Put two the halves together to make a circle. Carefully, making sure you don't lose any ends, cut around the outside of the circle.

3 Tie a loose end of yarn tightly around the middle of the pompom. Try to wrap it around another time and tie a knot again to ensure the pompom is tied securely.

4 Pull the pompom maker apart to create the pompom.

5 Trim any straggly ends of yarn to make a neat ball.

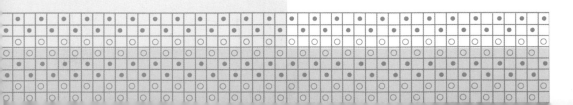

Tassels

Tassels are fun decorations for scarves and belts, and can be used to create plaits and fake hair.

2 Cut the bottom loop of the tassel and remove from cardboard carefully.

4 Pull the loop end a little way through the knitting.

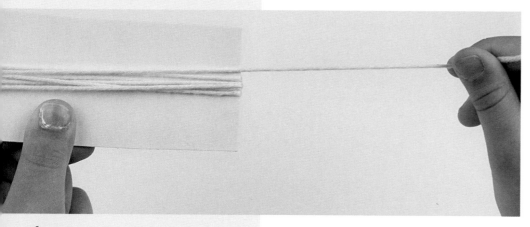

1 Wind some yarn around a piece of card, cut to the length you want your tassel to be. This will ensure all your tassel's ends are the same length.

3 Push a crochet hook through the knitting, where you want the tassel to be. Grab the loop end of the tassel with the hook.

5 Tuck the cut ends through the loop.

6 Pull the cut ends tight.

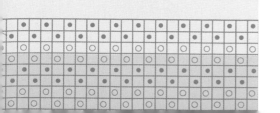

Warm and cozy knits

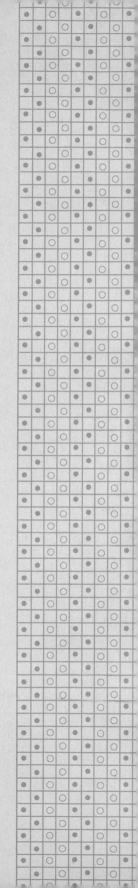

Skill Level

Cowl

It is hard to believe, but this pattern is even easier than a scarf because it is not as long and so won't take as much time to knit!

MEASUREMENTS

❶ One size, approx 18in (46cm) all around and 7¼in (18cm) wide

SKILL LEVEL

❶ Easy

YARN

❶ 1 x 3½oz (100g)—approx 98yd (90m)—Rico Yarns Fashion Super Chunky, 60% new wool, 40% acrylic, in shade 13 teal

ALTERNATIVE YARNS

❶ Any super-bulky weight yarn,

although you could use the same principle to make a cowl out of any yarn—just knit a strip then sew it into a loop. The cowl will just come out thinner or thicker depending on the yarn!

GAUGE (TENSION)

❶ 11 sts and 18 rows to 4in (10cm) in garter stitch using US 13 (9mm) needles

NOTIONS

❶ Pair of US 13 (9mm) needles
❶ Darning needle
❶ Ribbon to decorate, if desired

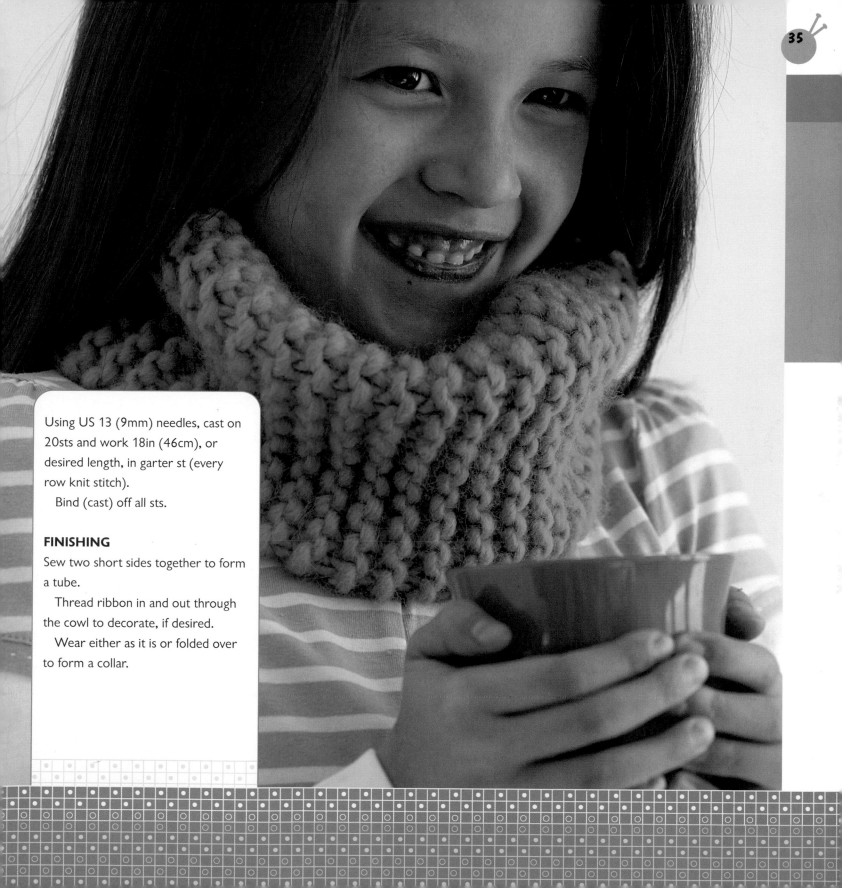

Using US 13 (9mm) needles, cast on 20sts and work 18in (46cm), or desired length, in garter st (every row knit stitch).

Bind (cast) off all sts.

FINISHING

Sew two short sides together to form a tube.

Thread ribbon in and out through the cowl to decorate, if desired.

Wear either as it is or folded over to form a collar.

Skill Level

Plait Hat

This very basic pattern is a great project to practice shaping and you can knit it plain or striped without embellishment. Add the plaits or spiky hair for a fun hat or for your dressing-up box.

MEASUREMENTS

❷ S, M, L, to fit head up to 18(20:22)in (46(51:56)cm)

SKILL LEVEL

❷ Intermediate

YARN

❷ **Yarn A**: 1(2:2) x 1¾oz (50g)—approx 180yd (165m)—Rico : Baby Classic Aran, 50% acrylic, 50% polyamide, in shade 9755 pink

❷ **Yarn B**: 1 x 1¾oz (50g)—approx 137yd (125m)—Millamia Merino, 100% merino, in shade 142 daisy yellow

ALTERNATIVE YARNS

❷ Any worsted/Aran weight yarn is fine for this hat, but you can use whatever different yarns you wish for the hair—try textured yarns for curly hair, or bright colors for punk-style hair!

GAUGE (TENSION)

❷ 18 sts and 24 rows to 4in (10cm) in stockinette (stocking) stitch using US 8 (5mm) needles

NOTIONS

❷ Pair each of US 7 (4.5mm) and US 8 (5mm) needles
❷ Darning needle
❷ Cardboard to make plaits

Using US 7 (4.5mm) needles and yarn A, cast on 82(90:98) sts.

Row 1: k2, [p2, k2] to end of row.

Row 2: p2, [k2, p2] to end of row.

   Repeat last two rows twice more. (Six rows worked.)

   Change to larger needles and continue as folls:

Row 7: knit.

Row 8: purl.

   Continue in stockinette (stocking) stitch as rows 7 and 8 until hat measures 5½(6:6)in (14(15:15)cm) from cast-on edge.

Decrease for Crown

Row 1: [k4, k2tog] to last 4(0:2) stitches, k4(0:2). (69(75:82) sts)

Row 2: purl.

Row 3: knit.

Row 4: purl.

Row 5: [k3, k2tog] to last 4(0:2) stitches, k4(0:2).
(56(60:66) sts)

Row 6: purl.

Row 7: [k2, k2tog] to last 4(0:2) stitches, k4(0:2).
(43(45:50) sts)

Row 8: purl.

Row 9: [k1, k2tog] to last 4(0:2) stitches, k4(0:2).
(30(30:34) sts)

Row 10: purl.

Row 11: [k2tog] to end of row. (15(15:17) sts)

Row 12: purl.

Do not bind (cast) off, but cut yarn, leaving a long tail.
Using a darning needle, thread tail through remaining
15[15:17] sts and pull up tight to gather into a circle. Sew
up side seam using mattress stitch. Weave in all ends.

PLAITS

Cut a piece of cardboard to 16in (40cm) long. Wrap yarn B
around cardboard 12 times, starting at bottom. Cut loops at
bottom of cardboard and take off yarn, folded in half. Insert
a length of yarn through loop at top and tie in place to hold
yarn together. Ask a friend to hold the top loop while you
plait. Split the 24 ends of yarn into 3 equal sections and plait
the length, tying a knot in the bottom to secure.

Make another plait in the same way.

FINISHING

Sew one plait on either side of hat, to the inside of rib, with
seam at the back.

 ## Skill Level

Snake Scarf

Knitting a scarf can be boring, but this pattern certainly isn't! Use the basic scarf pattern with a head at one end and a tail at the other to create your own animal using felt, buttons, and fabric.

MEASUREMENTS

❂ One size—you can customize the length to fit you, but the scarf is approx 5in (12.5cm) wide

SKILL LEVEL

❂ Intermediate

YARN

❂ 1¾oz (50g)—approx 294yd (270m)—Debbie Bliss Cashmerino Aran, 55% merino wool, 33% microfiber, 12% cashmere, in:

Snake

❂ **Yarn A:** 2 x shade 502 lime

❂ **Yarn B:** 1 x shade 034 yellow

Cat

❂ **Yarn A:** 2 x shade 003 orange

❂ **Yarn B:** 1 x shade 009 gray

ALTERNATIVE YARNS

❂ Any Aran/worsted weight yarn will do, but you can use different thickness yarns and change your needles to match, the scarf will just come out bigger or smaller!

GAUGE (TENSION)

❂ Not essential, but 18 sts and 24 rows to 4in (10cm) in seed (moss) stitch using US 7 (4.5mm) needles is good

NOTIONS

❂ Pair of US 7 (4.5mm) needles

❂ Buttons for eyes

❂ Felt for tongue and ears or other features

❂ Darning needle

❂ Sewing needle and thread

Using US 7 (4.5mm) needles and yarn A, cast on 3 sts.

Row 1: k1, p1, k1.

Row 2: inc1, p1, inc1. (5 sts)

Row 3: p1, [k1, p1] to end of row.

Row 4: inc1, k1, p1, k1, inc1. (7 sts)

Row 5: k1, [p1, k1] to end of row. Seed (moss) pattern is set.

Row 6: inc1, p1, work seed (moss) st to last st, inc1. (9 sts)

Row 7: p1, [k1, p1] to end of row.

Row 8: inc1, k1, work seed (moss) st to last st, inc1. (11 sts)

Row 9: k1, [p1, k1] to end of row.

Row 10: inc1, p1, work seed (moss) st to last st, inc1. (13 sts)

Row 11: p1, [k1, p1] to end of row.

Row 12: inc1, k1, work seed (moss) st to last st, inc1. (15 sts)

Row 13: k1, [p1, k1] to end of row.

Row 14: inc1, p1, work seed (moss) st to last st, inc1. (17 sts)

Row 15: p1, [k1, p1] to end of row.

Row 16: inc1, k1, work seed (moss) st to last st, inc1. (19 sts)

Row 17: k1, [p1, k1] to end of row.

Row 18: inc1, p1, work seed (moss) st to last st, inc1. (21 sts)

Row 19: p1, [k1, p1] to end of row.

Row 20: inc1, k1, work seed (moss) st to last st, inc1. (23 sts)

Row 21: k1, [p1, k1] to end of row.

Repeat row 21 for 2¼in (6cm).

Change to yarn B and work 2¼in (6cm) as row 21.

Change to yarn A and work 2¼in (6cm) as row 21.

Continue working as row 21, changing color every 2¼in (6cm) until scarf measures approximately 1yd (1m), ending with a yarn B stripe.

Change to yarn A and work 4 rows in pattern.

Shape Head

Row 1: increase one stitch at either end of row, keeping to seed (moss) stitch as established. (25 sts)

Row 2: work straight in seed (moss) stitch.

Repeat last two rows until you have 31 sts.

Work straight in seed (moss) stitch pattern for 15 rows.

Next row: k2tog, work in seed (moss) stitch to last two sts, k2tog. (29 sts)

Next row: work straight in seed (moss) stitch.

Repeat last two rows until you have 17 sts.

Bind (cast) off all stitches.

FINISHING

Attach buttons to head for eyes.

Cut out a piece of felt into a forked tongue shape and sew to bottom of head for snake.

For cat, cut out some felt ears and a felt tongue and sew these to head. Stitch on a nose and mouth and add whiskers if you wish!

Skill Level

Earmuffs

If you don't like hats but can't stand having cold ears, earmuffs are for you—and they are great for when your friends just talk too loudly!

MEASUREMENTS
- One size, approx18in (46cm) from bottom of one ear to bottom of other

SKILL LEVEL
- Easy

YARN
- 1 x 1¾oz (50g)—approx 98yd (90m)—of Patons Fairytale Dreamtime DK, 100% pure wool, in each of:
- **Yarn A:** shade 4953 pink
- **Yarn B:** shade 4954 lilac
- **Yarn C:** shade 4957 turquoise
- **Yarn D:** shade 4952 lime
- **Yarn E:** shade 4960 yellow

ALTERNATIVE YARNS
- Any DK or sportweight yarn will do to achieve the same size earmuffs; choose something very warm, soft and cozy!

GAUGE (TENSION)
- 22 sts and 30 rows to 4in (10cm) in stockinette (stocking) stitch using US 6 (4mm) needles

NOTIONS
- Pair of US 6 (4mm) needles
- Darning needle
- Toy stuffing

Using US 6 (4mm) needles and yarn A, cast on 63 sts.

Row 1: purl.

Change to yarn B.

Row 2: [k7, k2tog] to end of row. (56 sts)

Row 3 (and every alt row): purl.

Row 4: [k6, k2tog] to end of row. (49 sts)

After the next purl row, change to yarn C.

Row 6: [k5, k2tog] to end of row. (42 sts)

Row 8: [k4, k2tog] to end of row. (35 sts)

After the next purl row, change to yarn D.

Row 10: [k3, k2tog] to end of row. (28 sts)

Row 12: [k2, k2tog] to end of row. (21 sts)

After the next purl row, change to yarn E.

Row 14: [k1, k2tog] to end of row. (14 sts)

Row 16: [k2tog] to end of row. (7 sts)

Thread yarn through remaining sts and pull up to form circle, sew up side seam.

Make one further piece in this way, then two further pieces entirely in yarn E, for the back of earmuff, without striping.

Sew one striped circle to one plain circle—so that both right sides face outward—all around circumference, leaving a small gap for stuffing. Fill with toy stuffing to desired fullness and sew up gap.

Do the same with two remaining circles.

BAND

Using US 6 (4mm) needles and yarn A cast on 12 sts and work in garter st, in two row stripes alternately of yarns A, B, C, D, and E until band measures 10in (25cm).

Bind (cast) off.

TIES

Finger-knit two lengths of chain approx 19¾in (50cm) long.

To finger-knit, make a slip knot and place it on your pointy/forefinger. Wrap another loop of yarn around your finger, closer to the end of the finger. Pull the slip knot over the second loop and off your finger, without dropping second loop—like binding (casting) off. Wrap another loop of yarn around your finger, closer to the end. Pull first loop over second loop and off your finger, without dropping second loop. Repeat for entire length of finger-knitting.

FINISHING

Sew an earmuff to either end of the band, with all right sides facing out.

Attach a tie to bottom of either earmuff to fasten under chin with a bow.

Snowday Earflap Hat

A multicolored hat to cheer you up and keep you
warm on cold and dreary days. This yarn changes color as
you knit, giving you the illusion of stripes without
you having to change yarns—easy!

MEASUREMENTS

❸ L is up to 19¾in (50cm) head
M is up to 21¼in (54cm) head

SKILL LEVEL

❸ Intermediate

YARN

❸ 2(2) x 1¾oz (50g)—approx
190yd (174m)—Crystal Palace
Yarns, Mochi Plus, 80% merino
wool, 20% nylon, in shade 551
intense rainbow

ALTERNTIVE YARNS

❸ Any Aran weight yarn will do,
you can stripe up a few different
shades if you cannot find a
variegated yarn that stripes itself.
Wool or a wool mix yarn is great
here for warmth

GAUGE (TENSION)

❸ 18 sts and 24 rows to 4in
(10cm) in stockinette (stocking)
stitch using US 8 (5mm) needles

NOTIONS

❸ Pair of US 8 (5mm) needles
❸ Stitch holders
❸ Darning needle

EARFLAPS (MAKE TWO)

Using US 8 (5mm) needles, cast on 6 sts.
Row 1(WS): purl.
Row 2: inc1, k to last st, inc1.
　Repeat last two rows until there are 18 sts.
Next row: purl.
　Leave each earflap on a stitch holder.

HAT

Using US 8 (5mm) needles, cast on 12(14) sts, knit across
18 sts from first earflap with right side facing, cast on 32(36),
knit across 18 sts from second earflap with right side facing,
cast on 12(14) sts. (92(100) sts)
Row 1(WS): purl across all sts.
Row 2: knit.
　Continue in st st in this way on these 92(100) sts until work
measures 4¾in (12cm) (5½in (14cm)) from cast-on brim,
ending with a purl row.

Decrease for Crown

Row 1: [k4, k2tog] to last 2(4) sts, k2(4). (77(84) sts)

Beginning with a p row, work 3 rows st st.

Row 5: [k3, k2tog] to last 2(4) sts, k2(4). (62(68) sts)

Beginning with a p row, work 3 rows st st.

Row 9: [k2, k2tog] to last 2(4) sts, k2(4). (47(52) sts)

Row 10 (and every other row): purl.

Row 11: [k1, k2tog] to last 2(4) sts, k2(4). (32(36) sts

Row 13: [k2tog] to end of row. (16(18) sts)

Work in st st on these sts for 1¼in (3cm).

K2tog to end of row. (8(9) sts)

Thread yarn through remaining sts, pull up tight.

FINISHING

Rejoin yarn to one end of lower edge. With right side facing, pick up and knit 107[115] sts all along edge.

Row 1(WS): [k1, p1] to last st, k1.

Row 2: [p1, k1] to last st, p1.

Repeat rows 1–2 once more.

Bind (cast) off loosely in rib. Sew up side seam.

Skill Level

Alpine Adventures Balaclava

A great pattern for keeping your ears,
head, and neck warm.

MEASUREMENTS
- To fit 6–8(9–10) yrs

SKILL LEVEL
- Difficult

YARN
- 2 x 1¾oz (50g)—approx
262yd (240m)—Rico
Essentials Merino DK,
100% merino wool, in shade
39 petrol

ALTERNATIVE YARNS
- Any DK weight yarn will
do, you can also stripe the
balaclava or knit the ribbing

in a different color for a
different look

GAUGE (TENSION)
- 22 sts and 28 rows to 4in
(10cm) in stockinette
(stocking) stitch using US 6
(4mm) needles

NOTIONS
- Pair each of US 3
(3.25mm) and US 6
(4mm) needles
- Stitch holder
- Darning needle

Using US 6 (4mm) needles,
cast on 73(83) sts.
Row 1(RS): k2, [p1, k1] to
last st, k1.
Row 2: p2, [k1, p1] to last st, p1.
  Repeat last two rows for ¾in (2cm), ending with a row 2.
  Change to US 3 (3.25mm) needles and continue in rib as
rows one and two until work measures 2¼(2¾)in (6(7)cm)
ending with a row 2.
Next row: rib to last 9(11) sts. Turn. Leave these 9(11) sts
on a stitch holder, unworked.
Next row: rib across to to last 9(11) sts. Turn. Leave these
9(11) sts on another stitch holder, unworked. (55(61) sts)
Next row: rib 3, *inc1, rib 6(5); repeat from * to last 3(4)
sts, inc1, rib to end. (63(71) sts)
Next row: purl.
  Change to US 6 (4mm) needles.
Row 1: knit.

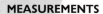

Row 2: purl.

Continue in stockinette (stocking) stitch in this way until work measures 9(10¾)in (23(27)cm) from cast on edge, ending with a purl row.

Next row: bind (cast) off 21(24) sts, k to end.

Next row: bind (cast) off 21(24) sts, p to end.

Continue in stockinette (stocking) stitch on these remaining 21(23) sts until this center panel is as long as the edges just bound (cast) off.

Bind (cast) off all sts.

FINISHING

Sew sides of center panel into position along bound- (cast-) off edges.

Border

With right side facing and US 3 (3.25mm) needles, slip first 9(11) sts from stitch holder onto needle, rejoin yarn, pick up and knit 41(43) sts along side panel, 19(21) sts along center panel, 41(43) sts along other side panel, then rib across sts on second holder. (119(129) sts)

Starting with a row 2, work 7(9) rows of rib as for rows 1–2 of projct.

Bind (cast) off all sts in rib.

Sew up neck seam.

Skill Level

Mouse Mittens

These mittens will keep you warm and act as a toy at the same time. Have your own puppet show and make each hand a different animal!

MEASUREMENTS
- To fit 6-8(9-11) yrs

SKILL LEVEL
- Difficult

YARN
- 1(1) x 1¾oz (50g)—approx 131yd (120m)—Artesano Inca Cloud, 100% alpaca, in each of:
- **Yarn A:** shade ZK gray
- **Yarn B:** shade B432 pink

ALTERNATIVE YARNS
- Any DK or sportweight yarn will do. Try a warm and fluffy yarn and/or a mix of natural with man-made fibers for the warmth and durability that mittens need. You can use all kinds of scraps of yarn for the embellishments, using different colors and textures for animals you may wish to create

GAUGE (TENSION)
- 24 sts and 32 rows to 4in (10cm) in stockinette (stocking) stitch using US 5 (3.75mm) needles

NOTIONS
- Pair each of US 3 (3.25mm) and US 5 (3.75mm) needles
- Darning needle
- Buttons for eyes

Using US 3 (3.25mm) needles and yarn A, cast on 41(45) sts.
Row 1(RS): k2, [p1, k1] to last st, k1.
Row 2: p2, [k1, p1] to last st, p1.
  Repeat these two rows until rib measures 1½in (4cm), ending with a row 2.
  Change to larger needles and st st and work 6(8) rows st st, beginning with a k row.

Increase for Thumb
Row 1: k19(21), inc into next st, k1, inc into next st, k to end. (43(47) sts)
Row 2 (and every even row): purl.
Row 3: k19(21), inc into next st, k3, inc into next st, k to end. (45(49) sts)
Row 5: k19(21), inc into next st, k5, inc into next st, k to end. (47(51) sts)
  Continue to inc for thumb gusset in this way until you have 49(55) sts, ending with a k row.
Next row: purl.

Next row: k30(34), cast on 1 st, turn, leaving remaining sts unworked.

Next row: p12(14), cast on 1 st, turn and continue to work just on these 13(15) sts for 1½in (4cm), ending with a p row.

Shape Thumb Top

Next row: [k1, k2tog] to last 1(0) st, k1(0). (9(10) sts)

Next row: purl.

Next row: k1(0), [k2tog] to end. (5 sts)

Break off yarn and thread through remaining sts, pull up tightly and secure, sew up thumb seam.

Hand

With RS facing, rejoin yarn, pick up and knit 3 sts along base of thumb, knit remaining 19(21) unworked sts on left-hand needle.

Purl across all sts. (41(45) sts)

Work in st st for 2(2¼)in (5(6)cm) ending with a p row.

Shape Top

Row 1: [k1, k2tog, k15(17), k2tog] twice, k1. (37(41) sts)

Row 2 (and every even row): purl.

Row 3: [k1, k2tog, k13(15), k2tog] twice, k1. (33(37) sts)

Row 5: [k1, k2tog, k11(13), k2tog] twice, k1. (29(33) sts)

Row 7: [k1, k2tog, k9(11), k2tog] twice, k1. (25(29) sts)

Continue dec 4 sts every row as established until you have 17 sts.

Break off yarn and thread through remaining sts, pull up tightly and secure, sew up side seam.

OUTER EARS

Using US 5 (3.75mm) needles and yarn A, cast on 5 sts.

Row 1: knit.

Row 2: purl.

Row 3: inc1, k to last st, inc1. (7 sts)

Row 4: purl.

Row 5: inc1, k to last st, inc1. (9 sts)

Work three rows st st.

Row 9: k2tog, k to last 2 sts, k2tog. (7 sts)

Row 10: purl.

Row 11: k2tog, k to last 2 sts, k2tog. (5 sts)

Row 12: purl.

　Bind (cast) off all sts.

　Make three more pieces the same.

INNER EARS

Using US 5 (3.75mm) needles and yarn B, cast on 5 sts.

Rows 1–2: knit.

Row 3: inc1, k to last st, inc1. (7 sts)

Row 4: knit.

Row 5: inc1, k to last st, inc1. (9 sts)

　Work four rows garter st (knit every row).

Row 10: ktog, k to last 2 sts, k2tog. (7 sts)

Row 11: knit.

Row 12: ktog, k to last 2 sts, k2tog. (5 sts)

Row 13: knit.

　Bind (cast) off all sts.

　Make three more pieces the same.

FINISHING

Sew each yarn A st st circle to a yarn B, garter st circle, with RS of st st piece on the outside.

　Sew two ears to each mitten, to the top side.

　Attach two small buttons for eyes to each mitten and embroider a nose and, if you wish, whiskers and other embellishments.

Accessories

- 🐑 Pompom necklace
- 🐑 Tassel belt
- 🐑 Hair band
- 🐑 Flowers
- 🐑 Little bows
- 🐑 Bling bracelets and necklace
- 🐑 Decorative buttons
- 🐑 Legwarmers
- 🐑 School bag
- 🐑 Fingerless mitts
- 🐑 Pretty slippers

Skill Level

Pompom Necklace

Feel like a princess in this easy-to-make, fun-to-wear necklace. Use up your scraps of yarn from other projects to make the pompoms in whatever color mix you like. Here, the ends of balls from the zigzag cushion have been used to create the pompom beads. Make some French knitting bracelets to match!

MEASUREMENTS
- One size, approx 12in (30cm) drop

SKILL LEVEL
- Difficult

YARN
- 1 x 1¾oz (50g)—approx 127yd (116m)—of Sublime Cashmere Merino Silk DK, 75% extra fine merino, 20% silk, 5% cashmere, in each of:
- **Yarn A:** shade 119 lido
- **Yarn B:** shade 124 splash
- **Yarn C:** shade 194 seesaw
- **Yarn D:** shade 195 puzzle
- **Yarn E:** shade 122 honeybunny
- **Yarn F:** shade 158 ladybug

ALTERNATIVE YARNS
- Use any yarn you wish for the necklace, using up scraps of yarn or mixing weights to create different-sized pompoms

GAUGE (TENSION)
- Not necessary

NOTIONS
- Pompom makers, various sizes, here they were ¾in (2cm) and 1in (2.5cm) in diameter
- French knitting bobbin
- Darning needle

NECKLACE

Make eight pompom beads (or the amount you wish) in varying sizes

Finger-knit (see page 41) a chain of approx 24in (61cm). Thread the pompom beads onto the chain, using the darning needle to thread the chain straight through the center of each pompom, then tie the chain into a circle.

BRACELETS

Using a French knitting bobbin according to the instructions on the pack make lengths of French knitting long enough to go around the widest part of your hand and sew into a loop.

You can make some pieces long enough for necklaces, too.

Skill Level

Tassel Belt

This is a perfect pattern for total beginners, using only the simplest knit stitch and some stripes to great effect. Make the belt and tassels as long as you wish.

MEASUREMENTS

❷ One size—you can customize the length to fit you, but the belt is approx 2¼in (6cm) wide

SKILL LEVEL

❷ Easy

YARN

❷ 1 x 1¾oz (50g)—approx 246yd (225m)—Debbie Bliss Eco Aran, 100% organic cotton, in each of:

❷ **Yarn A:** shade 620 lime

❷ **Yarn B:** shade 609 purple

❷ **Yarn C:** shade 621 jade

GAUGE (TENSION)

❷ 18 sts and 28 rows to 4in (10cm) in garter stitch using US 7 (4.5mm) needles

NOTIONS

❷ Pair of US 7 (4.5mm) needles

❷ A small crochet hook to pull through tassels

❷ Cardboard to make tassels

❷ Darning needle

Using US 7 (4.5mm) needles and yarn A, cast on 10 sts.

Row 1: knit.

Row 2: knit.

   Change to yarn B.

Row 3: knit.

Row 4: knit.

   Change to yarn C.

Row 5: knit.

Row 6: knit.

   Change to yarn A.

   Repeat these 6 rows, changing color every two rows until belt is desired length—enough to go round your waist and tie up—ending with two rows of yarn A.

   Bind (cast) off all sts and weave in ends.

TASSELS

Cut a piece of cardboard to 4¾in (12cm) long (or desired length of tassel).

   Wind yarn A round the cardboard five times, starting from the bottom of the card. Cut the loops at the bottom of the tassel and remove from card, still folded in half.

   Insert crochet hook through the bottom right-hand corner of one end of belt and pull the looped end of tassel through for approx ½in (1cm). Pass the cut end of the tassel through the looped end and pull to secure. Repeat this twice more at even intervals along short end of belt, then repeat at opposite end.

   Trim tassels to the same length.

Skill Level

Hair Band

A very easy, pretty and practical way of tidying your hair. Make lots of them to match your favorite outfits.

MEASUREMENTS
- To fit approx 19¾(20½:21¼)in (50(52:54)cm) head

SKILL LEVEL
- Easy

YARN
- 1 x 1¾oz (50g)—approx 127yd (115m)—of Twilleys Freedom Cotton DK, 100% organic cotton, in each of:
- **Yarn A:** 606 raspberry
- **Yarn B:** 605 wild rose

ALTERNATIVE YARNS
- Any DK weight yarn will be perfect for this project, and something that has a bit of elastic in may do even better!

GAUGE (TENSION)
- 22 sts and 28 rows to 4in (10cm) in stockinette (stocking) stitch using US 6 (4mm) needles

NOTIONS
- Pair of US 6 (4mm) needles
- Darning needle

Using US 6 (4mm) needles and yarn A, cast on 83(89:95) sts.

Row 1: k1, [p1, k1] to end of row.

Row 2: p1, [k1, p1] to end of row.

   Change to yarn B and repeat last two rows.

   Change to yarn A.

   Repeat last 4 rows once more, then repeat rows 1–2 in yarn A.

   Bind (cast) off all sts.

FINISHING

Sew two short ends together to form a loop. Sew in all ends.

Skill Level

Flowers

You only need basic knit stitch for this project, although you could knit flowers in whatever stitch you like. The yarn thickness does not matter, as the flowers will just be bigger or smaller depending on what you use. Pop flowers on hair grips, alice bands, brooch backs, and more, and embellish them with buttons and ribbons for versatile accessories.

MEASUREMENTS

❶ Small (large) sizes
These vary depending on yarn, needle size, and how tightly you roll them when making up, but they are approximately 2–3in (5–7.5cm) in diameter

SKILL LEVEL

❶ Easy

YARN

❶ Use any scraps of yarn left over from your other projects—these flowers do not take much yarn. You could also stripe them up with lots of short leftover lengths of yarn. We have used a variety of different Aran/worsted weight yarns from the other projects in the book.

GAUGE (TENSION)

❶ Not necessary

NOTIONS

❶ We used US 8 (5mm) needles to go with our Aran/worsted weight yarn, but you can use whichever needles the ball band of the yarn you are using asks for
❶ Buttons to decorate as desired
❶ Brooch back/hair grip/safety pin for fastening
❶ Darning needle
❶ Sewing needle and thread

Using US 8 (5mm) needles and Aran weight yarn, cast on 50(70) sts and knit every row (garter stitch) for 6–10 rows, until the flower is about half the diameter you want it, adding stripes of different colors if you wish.

Don't bind (cast) off, but cut your yarn, leaving enough to sew up, thread the tail through all stitches on needle, and pull up gently to gather the flower as much as you wish.

Curl the strip around on itself into a coil and secure with some stitches at the back to hold it in shape.

FINISHING

Decorate as desired with a button and/or ribbons, sewing buttons to the front and ribbons around the back.

Attach the sort of fastening you want at the back—for example, a safety pin or brooch back to make a brooch or corsage.

Skill Level

Little Bows

Bows to put in your hair or wear as brooches. The shiny yarn is very pretty and the pattern is so easy that you can even play with the stitch used to make bows with different textures

MEASUREMENTS

❷ One size, approx 2¾in (7cm) wide

SKILL LEVEL

❷ Easy

YARN

❷ 1 x 1¾oz (50g)—approx 127yd (116m)—Sublime Cashmere Merino Silk DK, 75% extra fine merino, 20% silk, 5% cashmere, in each of:

❷ **Yarn A:** shade 208 neroli

❷ **Yarn B:** shade 209 organdie

❷ **Yarn C:** shade 210 Thai tea

❷ **Yarn D:** shade 212 saffron

❷ **Yarn E:** shade 214 kimono

ALTERNATIVE YARNS

❷ Any DK weight yarn will do here, but you could try any yarn; bows will just come out different sizes. The yarn used here is silky, but you could try a matt yarn, or a mixture of shiny and matt for different textures

GAUGE (TENSION)

❷ 22 sts and 32 rows to 4in (10cm) in garter using US 6 (4mm) needles

NOTIONS

❷ Pair of US 6 (4mm) needles

❷ Darning needle

❷ Safety pins/brooch backs

❷ Hair grips/headbands

❷ Sewing needle and thread

Using US 6 (4mm) needles, cast on 10 sts and work in garter st (every row knit) for 5½in (14cm) or twice desired length for bow.

Bind (cast) off.

Sew short ends together to form a loop.

Using US 6 (4mm) needles, cast on 5 sts and work in st st (one row knit, one row purl) for 10 rows.

Bind (cast) off.

FINISHING

Wrap st st strip around middle of garter st loop and sew together short ends at back.

Sew a hairgrip, brooch back or safety pin to back of bow.

Make up the bows in different colors, or mix and match the colors of bow and tie sections, or even stripe the bows for differing styles.

 **Skill Level**

Bling Bracelets and Necklace

When you get a little bored of your knitting, put it down and have a break to French knit this quick-and-easy jewellery, perfect for gifts, or just to wear yourself!

MEASUREMENTS

❷ One size

SKILL LEVEL

❷ Intermediate

YARN

❷ 1 x 1¾oz (50g)—approx 127yd (116m)—of Sublime Cashmere Merino Silk DK, 75% extra fine merino, 20% silk, 5% cashmere, in each of:

❷ **Yarn A:** shade 124 splash

❷ **Yarn B:** shade 194 seesaw

❷ **Yarn C:** shade 009 pink

❷ **Yarn D:** shade td53 purple

ALTERNATIVE YARNS

❷ Any DK or sportweight yarn will do, although you could use any weight of yarn and and change the size of the jewels to suit it

GAUGE (TENSION)

❷ Not necessary

NOTIONS

❷ French knitting bobbin

❷ Darning needle

❷ Assorted beads, sequins or buttons for added "bling"

❷ Sewing needle and thread

Following the instructions included with the bobbin, French knit a length of tube long enough to either wear around your wrist or to the desired length of necklace.

Fasten off the tube according to the instructions on the pack.

Sew the two ends of tube together to form a loop. Sew on desired beads and embellishments for the amount of "bling" you require.

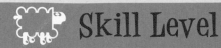

Decorative Buttons

Use up all your scraps making these bright and beautiful covered buttons that you can use on your clothes instead of your boring old buttons, or as badges on coats and bags.

MEASUREMENTS

❶ Buttons used are 1½in (38mm), 1¼in (29mm), 7/8in (23mm) and 5/8in (15mm)

SKILL LEVEL

❶ Easy

YARN

❶ Oddments of yarn from all the DK/worsted weight projects in the book

GAUGE (TENSION)

❶ Not essential but roughly 22 sts and 28 rows to 4in (10cm) in stockinette (stocking) stitch using US 6 (4mm) needles

NOTIONS

❶ Pair of US 6 (4mm) needles

❶ Darning needle

❶ Self-cover buttons kit

LARGE BUTTON

Using US 6 (4mm) needles and any yarn, cast on 11 sts and work in st st until piece is square, striping colors as desired.

Bind (cast) off all sts.

MEDIUM BUTTONS

Using US 6 (4mm) needles and any yarn, cast on 8 sts and work in st st until piece is square, striping colors as desired.

Bind (cast) off all sts.

SMALL BUTTONS

Using US 6 (4mm) needles and any yarn, cast on 5 sts and work in st st until piece is square, striping colors as desired.

Bind (cast) off all sts.

Cover all buttons with the squares of knitting, following the instructions on the kit.

Sew to garments or accessories as decoration, or in place of existing buttons.

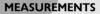

Legwarmers

These legwarmers are great for keeping you warm in winter or for wearing to dance or gym classes.

MEASUREMENTS

- To fit approx 8¼(9:10)in (21(23:25)cm) calf; you can make the legwarmers as long or as short as you wish

SKILL LEVEL

- Easy

YARN

- 1 x 1¾oz (50g)—approx 196yd (180m)—Debbie Bliss Cashmerino Aran, 55% merino wool, 33% microfiber, 12% cashmere, in each of:
- **Yarn A**: shade 31 dark purple
- **Yarn B**: shade 17 light Purple

ALTERNATIVE YARNS

- Any worsted/Aran weight yarn is fine for these legwarmers

GAUGE (TENSION)

- 18 sts and 24 rows to 4in (10cm) in stockinette (stocking) stitch using US 8 (5mm) needles

NOTIONS

- Pair each of US 7 (4.5mm) and US 8 (5mm) needles
- Darning needle

Using US 7 (4.5mm) needles and yarn A, cast on 37(41:45) sts.

Row 1: k1, [p1, k1] to end of row.

Row 2: p1, [k1, p1] to end of row.

Repeat rib rows 1–2 until work measures 4in (10cm) from cast on, ending with a row 2.

Change to US 8 (5mm) needles and yarn B.

Next row: knit.

Next row: purl.

Continue in stockinette (stocking) stitch as last two rows until stockinette (stocking) stitch section measures 6in (15cm), or to desired leg length, ending with a purl row.

Change back to US 7 (4.5mm) needles and yarn A.

Next row: k1, [p1, k1] to end of row.

Next row: p1, [k1, p1] to end of row.

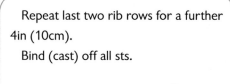

Repeat last two rib rows for a further 4in (10cm).

Bind (cast) off all sts.

FINISHING

Sew up long side seam of each legwarmer using whip stitch.

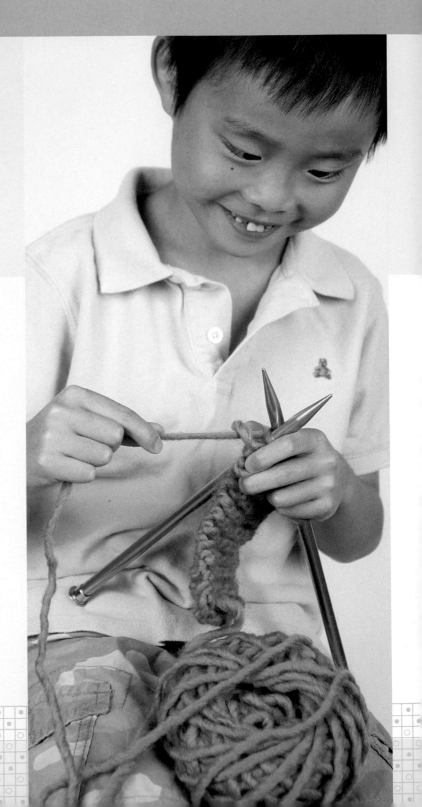

Skill Level

School Bag

A handy bag to hold all your stationary for school, or your goodies on a day out.

MEASUREMENTS

❷ One size, approx 12¼in wide by 8in deep (31cm wide by 20cm deep)

SKILL LEVEL

❷ Intermediate

YARN

❷ 1 x 3½oz (100g)— approx 196yd (180m)— Rico Fashion Super Chunky, 60% new wool, 40% acrylic, in each of:

❷ **Yarn A:** shade 04 navy

❷ **Yarn B:** shade 08 mustard

ALTERNATIVE YARNS

❷ Any super bulky weight yarn will work well

GAUGE (TENSION)

❷ 9 sts and 12 rows to 4in (10cm) in stockinette (stocking) stitch using US 15 (10mm) needles

NOTIONS

❷ Pair of US 15 (10mm) needles

❷ Darning needle

❷ Sewing needle and thread

❷ Fabric measuring 17¾ x 12in (45 x 30cm)

❷ Snap fastener

❷ Ribbon, if desired

Using US 15 (10mm) needles and yarn A, cast on 30 sts.

Row 1 (RS): knit.

Row 2: purl.

Continue in st st in this way until 17¾in (45cm) has been worked ending with a k row.

Change to yarn B and work 4 rows garter st (every row knit).

Bind (cast) off all sts.

STRAP

Using US 15 (10mm) needles and yarn B, cast on 5 sts and work approx 1yd (1m) in garter st (every row knit) or until desired strap length is worked.

Bind (cast) off all sts.

FINISHING

Turning under a narrow hem, slip stitch fabric to wrong side of bag piece, ensuring there is at least a ½in (1cm) gap to edge of knitting all around.

Fold over piece from bottom, to create an 8in (20cm) deep pouch. Sew up side seams.

Fold over top flap (with contrast stripe) and sew a snap fastener to the center of this flap on the wrong side, with corresponding part on right side of pouch.

Sew short ends of strap to either side of bag, along top of pouch.

Thread ribbon through stitches above stripe on flap if desired and tie into a bow.

Skill Level

Fingerless Mitts

Lots of people think knitting gloves is hard, but these mitts are just straight rectangles sewn up the side, so there is no excuse for not making them!
Knit them as long or short as you wish, depending on how warm you want your arms to be.

MEASUREMENTS

❶ S(M:L) to fit approx 6¾(7½:8¼)in (17(19:21)cm) wrist

SKILL LEVEL

❶ Easy

YARN

❶ 1 x 1¾oz (50g)—approx 131yd (120m)—Rico Essentials Merino DK, 100% merino wool, in each of:

Long gloves:

❶ **Yarn A**: shade 04 acacia
❶ **Yarn B**: shade 73 orange
❶ **Yarn C**: shade 66 sun

Short gloves:

❶ **Yarn A**: shade 38 dark blue
❶ **Yarn B**: shade 23 light blue
Yarn C: shade 18 bright blue

ALTERNATIVE YARNS

❶ Any DK weight yarn, you could use self-striping yarn if you can't be bothered to stripe different colors, or even do them in one color. A yarn which has some man-made fiber content— such as nylon or acrylic—

would be good, as these mitts will see a lot of wear and the man-made fiber will make them more durable

GAUGE (TENSION)

❶ 22 sts and 28 rows to 4in (10cm) in seed (moss) stitch using US 6 (4mm) needles

NOTIONS

❶ Pair each of US 5 (3.75mm) and US 6 (4mm) needles
Darning needle

Using US 5 (3.75mm) needles and yarn A, cast on 37(41:45) sts.
Row 1: k1, [p1, k1] to end of row.
Row 2: p1, [k1, p1] to end of row.
  Repeat last two rows for 1in (2.5cm) for short gloves, or 4¼in (11cm) for long gloves, or for desired length, ending with a row 2.
  Change to US 6 (4mm) needles and yarn B.
Row 1: knit.
Row 2: purl.
Change to yarn C.
Row 3: knit.
Row 4: purl.
  Change to yarn A.
Row 5: knit.
Row 6: purl.

Continue in stockinette (stocking) stitch (one row knit, one row purl) as for rows 1–6, changing color every two rows until striped section measures 2½(2¾:3¼)in (6(7:8)cm), ending with a purl row.

Change to US 5 (3.75mm) needles and yarn A.

Row 1: k1, [p1, k1] to end of row.

Row 2: p1, [k1, p1] to end of row.

Repeat these two rows once more.

Bind (cast) off all sts.

FINSHING

All lengths: sew up side seam on each glove from bottom of long rib to ½in (1cm) from beginning of striped section. Leave a gap of 1½in (4cm), and then sew up rest of seam to top of shorter rib.

Skill Level

Pretty Slippers

Slippers don't have to be boring, try these out for size! Customize them to make ballet slippers, ruby slippers, or even football boots.

MEASUREMENTS

❶ S[M:L] to fit foot approx 7(7¾:8¼)in (17.5(19.5:21)cm) long

SKILL LEVEL

❷ Intermediate

YARN

Ballet slippers

❶ 2(2:2) x 1¾oz (50g)—approx 127yd (116m)—of Sublime Cashmere Merino Silk DK, 75% extra fine merino, 20% silk, 5% cashmere, in shade 009 pink

Ruby slippers

❶ 2(2:2) x 1¾oz (50g)—approx 127yd (116m)—of Sublime Cashmere Merino Silk DK, 75% extra fine merino, 20% silk, 5% cashmere, in shade 192 teddy bear

ALTERNATIVE YARNS

❶ Any DK or sportweight yarn will do to achieve the same size slippers. It is best to use a yarn with at least a little man-made fiber in for durability. You could try some sock yarns.

GAUGE (TENSION)

❶ 22 sts and 28 rows to 4in (10cm) in stockinette (stocking) stitch using US 6 (4mm) needles

NOTIONS

❶ Pair of US 6 (4mm) needles
❶ Darning needle
❶ Ribbons
❶ Buttons

Basic Slipper Pattern

Using US 6 (4mm) needles cast on 22(25:28) sts.

Work in garter st (every row knit), increasing 1 st at either end of every alt row until there are 38(41:44) sts.

Work two rows straight.

Continue in garter st, decreasing 1 st at either end of every alt row until you are back to 22(25:28) sts.

Cast on 8(10:10) sts at beginning of next row for heel. (30(35:38) sts)

Continue in garter st, keeping heel edge straight and increasing 1 st at toe edge every alt row until there are 38(43:46) sts, ending at heel edge.

Bind (cast) off 20(25:28) sts, k to end. (18 sts)

Knit 13(15:15) further rows on remaining 18 sts, cast on 20(25:28) sts at end of last row. (38(43:46) sts)

Keeping heel straight, work on these sts, decreasing 1 st at toe edge on every alt row until 30(35:38) sts remain.

Bind (cast) off all sts.

Join heel seam and edges around sole, working in all fullness at toe.

Ruby slippers
STRAP (MAKE TWO)

Cast on 5 sts and work 4¼in (11cm) in garter st.

Next row: k2, yo, k2tog, k1.

Work in garter st until strap measures 4¾in (12cm).

Bind (cast) off all stitches.

Attach one strap to right inner ankle edge on first slipper and one to left inner ankle edge on second slipper.

Attach buttons to opposite sides top edge to align with buttonholes in straps.

Ballet Slippers.
HEEL TAB (MAKE TWO)

Cast on 8 sts and work 2½in (6cm) in garter st.

Bind (cast) off all sts.

Sew each tab into a loop at the top of heel. Thread a ribbon through each loop to tie around ankles.

Bedroom essentials

- Hot-water bottle cover
- Change purse
- MP3/phone cover
- Patchwork blanket
- Caterpillar doorstop
- Heart cushion
- Ladybug lavender bags
- Rainbow pillow cover

Skill Level

Hot-Water Bottle Cover

A simple rectangle can be made into a cute and cozy hot-water bottle cover that would make a pretty gift.

MEASUREMENTS

❷ One size, to fit an average hot-water bottle cover, approx 9in wide x 14in high (23cm wide x 36cm high)

SKILL LEVEL

❷ Easy

YARN

❷ 1 x 3½oz (100g)—approx 218yd (200m)—BC Garn Manu, 100% baby alpaca, in each of:
❷ **Yarn A:** shade un23 light teal
❷ **Yarn B:** shade un05 dark teal

ALTERNATIVE YARNS

❷ Any bulky weight yarn will do for this project. Try to find a soft and cozy yarn that you will enjoy cuddling and that will keep your bottle hot as long as possible

GAUGE (TENSION)

❷ 13 sts and 15 rows to 4in (10cm) in stockinette (stocking) stitch using US 11 (8mm) needles

NOTIONS

❷ Pair of US 11 (8 mm) needles
❷ Darning needle
❷ Approx 1yd (1m) of ½in (1cm) wide ribbon
❷ Hot-water bottle

Using US 11 (8mm) needles and yarn A, cast on 60 sts.

Work 3in (7.5cm) in garter st (every row knit).

Change to yarn B.

Next row: purl.

Next row: knit.

Continue in stockinette (stocking) stitch for 3in (7.5cm), ending with a purl row.

Change back to yarn A.

Work 8in (20cm) in garter st (every row knit).

Bind (cast) off all sts.

FINISHING

Fold rectangle in half widthways and sew up the bottom and side seam.

Thread ribbon in and out of the stitches all around, approx 2½in (6.5cm) down from opening.

Slip hot water bottle into the pouch made, pull up the ribbon and tie in a bow.

Skill Level

Change Purse

Keep all your loose change in this sweet purse and hide it away so your little brother or sister doesn't find it! Or use the purse to store favorite hair accessories and other treasures.

MEASUREMENTS

❶ One size, approx 4in (10cm) wide by 4in (10cm) tall

SKILL LEVEL

❶ Easy

YARN

❶ 1 x 1¾oz (50g)—approx 127yd (116m)—of Sublime Cashmere Merino Silk DK, 75% extra fine merino, 20% silk, 5% cashmere, in each of:

❶ **Yarn A**: shade 127 chicory

❶ **Yarn B**: shade 050 dilly

❶ **Yarn C**: shade 162 pinkaboo

ALTERNATIVE YARNS

❶ Any DK or sportweight yarn will achieve the same size purse, although you could use any weight of yarn and the purse will simply come out a different size

GAUGE (TENSION)

❶ 22 sts and 28 rows to 4in (10cm) in stockinette (stocking) stitch using US 6 (4mm) needles

NOTIONS

❶ Pair of US 6 (4mm) needles

❶ Darning needle

❶ Snap fastener

❶ Fabric 4 x 10in (10 x 23cm)

❶ Sewing needle and thread

Using US 6 (4mm) needles, and yarn A, cast on 25 sts.

Row 1(RS): k1, [p1, k1] to end of row.

Repeat last row five times more.

Change to yarn B, do not fasten off yarn A.

Next row: knit.

Change to yarn C, do not fasten off yarn B.

Next row: purl.

Continue in st st until work measures 9¼in (23.5cm), striping in one row stripes of yarns A, B, and C alternately, ending with a yarn C row.

Change to yarn A.

Next row: k1, [p1, k1] to end of row.

Repeat last row five times more.
  Bind (cast) off all sts.

FINISHING

Turning under a narrow hem, slip
stitch fabric to wrong side of knitted
strip between seed (moss) stitch
borders, leaving a gap of ¼in (0.5cm)
at knitting edges for sewing up purse.

  Fold strip up from bottom to create
pouch approx 4in (10cm) deep and
sew up side seam.

  Attach a snap fastener to flap and
main body of purse to close.

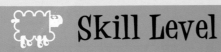

Skill Level

MP3/Phone Cover

A practical way to store your MP3 player
or phone so that it doesn't get knocked
around as you travel.

MEASUREMENTS

❂ One size, approx 4¾in
(12cm) long by 2in (5cm)
wide: will stretch to approx
2¾in (7cm) wide

SKILL LEVEL

❂ Easy

YARN

❂ 1 x 1¾oz (50g)—approx
137yd (125m)—Millamia
Merino, 100% merino, in
each of:

❂ **Yarn A**: shade 161
seaside

❂ **Yarn B**: shade 120
forget-me-not

ALTERNATIVE YARNS

❂ Any DK or sportweight
yarn will make a cover about
the same size as this one

GAUGE (TENSION)

❂ 30 sts and 30 rows to 4in
(10cm) in 1 x 1 rib using
US 3 (3.25mm) needles

NOTIONS

❂ Pair of US 3 (3.25mm)
needles

❂ Darning needle

❂ Button approx ¾in (2cm)
in diameter

Using US 3 (3.25mm) needles and yarn A, cast on 31 sts and
work in rib as folls:

Row 1(RS): k2, [p1, k1] to last st, k1.

Row 2: p2, [k1, p1] to last st, p1.

Change to yarn B and work 2 rows in rib, as rows 1–2.

Work 4¾in (12cm) in rib, alternating in stripes of yarn A
and B, ending with a row 1.

Next row: bind (cast) off 16 sts, rib to end of row. (15 sts)

Work on these 15 sts for 1½in (4cm), ending with a row 2.

Bind (cast) off all sts.

FINISHING

Fold piece widthways, with flap at top. Sew up bottom and
side seams.

Work 2¼in (6cm) of finger-knitting (see page 41) and attach
it to center of flap in a loop.

Attach button to main body of cover, corresponding to
finger-knitted loop.

Skill Level

Patchwork Blanket

A patchwork blanket made of squares is the perfect way to try out new stitches—just knit a different stitch in every swatch and sew them all together. It's easier to sew up if all the squares are the same size, but you can make them different sizes for a mismatched look.

MEASUREMENTS
- One size, each square approx 12 x 12in (30 x 30cm)

SKILL LEVEL
- Easy

YARN
- 1 x 3½oz (100g) BC Garn Tundra, 100% merino wool, in each of:
- **Yarn A**: shade td00 cream
- **Yarn B**: shade td02 light blue
- **Yarn C**: shade td06 pink

- **Yarn D**: shade td13 beige
- **Yarn E**: shade td16 yellow
- **Yarn F**: shade td18 green
- **Yarn G**: shade td53 purple

ALTERNATIVE YARNS
- Any bulky or super bulky yarn can be substituted, but if you just want to use up scraps of yarn to make a blanket, that is fine, too. Because a specific gauge (tension) is not necessary, you can just make the blanket whichever size you wish.

GAUGE (TENSION)
- 10 sts and 15 rows to 4in (10cm) in stockinette (stocking) stitch using US 13 (9mm) needles

NOTIONS
- Pair of US 13 (9mm) needles
- Darning needle

SQUARE ONE

Using US 13 (9mm) needles and any yarn you wish, cast on 30 sts.

Work 12in (30cm) in garter st (every row knit).

Bind (cast) off all sts.

SQUARE TWO

Using US 13 (9mm) needles and any yarn you wish, cast on 30 sts.

Work 12in (30cm) in stockinette (stocking) st (one row knit, one row purl).

Bind (cast) off all sts.

Make six of each square, in a mixture of colors, adding stripes if you wish.

FINISHING

To sew up the squares, lay them all
out flat and arrange as you like, with
three squares wide and four squares
long. Try to attach them with one
side edge to one cast-on or bound-
(cast-) off edge as this will help to
neaten the squares.

Using a contrast color of your
choice—either a left-over bit of yarn
from the squares or any other yarn
or thread—sew up the squares using
whip stitch.

Fasten off all ends and steam very
lightly into shape.

Skill Level

Caterpillar Doorstop

Use this cute caterpillar as a doorstop or draught excluder.

MEASUREMENTS

- One size, approx 26½in (67cm) long

SKILL LEVEL

- Intermediate

YARN

- 1 x 1¾oz (50g)—approx 87yd (80m)—Debbie Bliss Rialto Aran, 100% merino, in each of:
- **Yarn A:** shade 22 pale green
- **Yarn B:** shade 10 green
- **Yarn C:** shade 23 baby blue
- **Yarn D:** shade 08 purple

ALTERNATIVE YARNS

- Any Aran/worsted weight yarn will be work well; you could even use up old scraps of yarn and make a multicolored, stripy version

GAUGE (TENSION)

- 18 sts and 24 rows to 4in (10cm) in stockinette (stocking) stitch using US 8 (5mm) needles

NOTIONS

- Pair of US 8 (5mm) needles
- Darning needle
- Toy stuffing
- Pompom maker
- Buttons for eyes

BODY

Using US 8 (5mm) needles, and yarn A, cast on 5 sts.

Row 1 (and every other row): purl.

Row 2: knit twice into each st to end of row. (10 sts)

Row 4: knit twice into each st to end of row. (20 sts)

Row 6: [k1, inc1] to end of row. (30 sts)

Row 8: [k2, inc1] to end of row. (40 sts)

Row 10: [k3, inc1] to end of row. (50 sts)

Work ¾in (2cm) straight in yarn A.

Change to yarn B and work ¾in (2cm) straight.

Change to yarn C and work ¾in (2cm) straight.

Continue in st st in alternating ¾in (2cm) stripes of three colors until piece measures approx 25in (63.5cm), ending with a p row and a complete stripe.

Continue in color of next stripe only.

Next row: [k3, k2tog] to end of row. (40 sts)

Next row (and every other row): purl.

Next row: [k2, k2tog] to end of row. (30 sts)

Next row: [k1, k2tog] to end of row. (20 sts)

Next row: [k2tog] to end of row. (10 sts)

Next row: [k2tog] to end of row. (5 sts)

Do not bind (cast) off, but thread through remaining sts, pull up tight and secure in circle. Sew up side seam, leaving a gap to stuff. Stuff tube then sew up gap.

Thread yarn in and out all round tube approx 4in (10cm) down from one end, pull up to make head and secure. Repeat at other end for tail.

LEGS (MAKE EIGHT, OR MORE!!)

Using US 8 (5mm) needles and yarn D, cast on 8 sts.

Work ¾in (2cm) in garter st.

Bind (cast) off 4 sts, work straight in garter st on these 4 sts for a further ¾in (2cm).

Bind (cast) off all sts.

FINISHING

Attach legs along body, divided and spaced evenly on both sides between head and tail.

Make two pompoms and attach to head for antennae. Sew on two buttons for eyes, and embroider nose and smile in yarn D.

Heart Cushion

Who needs a boring old square cushion when you can decorate your bed with heart-shaped ones? These are also perfect gifts for moms on Mother's Day or Valentine's Day. You can vary how you stuff these cushions, making them sweet-smelling, lavender-filled sachets, mini beanbags, or squishy, soft pillows.

MEASUREMENTS
- One size, approx 7¼in (18cm) at widest point and 6¼in (16cm) tall

SKILL LEVEL
- Intermediate

YARN
- 1 x 1¾oz (50g)—approx 127yd (116m)—of Sublime Cashmere Merino Silk DK, 75% extra fine merino, 20% silk, 5% cashmere, in each of:
- **Yarn A:** shade 159 pansy
- **Yarn B:** shade 162 pinkaboo

ALTERNATIVE YARNS
- Any DK or sportweight yarn will do to achieve the same size cushion, although you could use any weight of yarn and the cushion will simply come out a different size

GAUGE (TENSION)
- 22 sts and 28 rows to 4in (10cm) in stockinette (stocking) stitch using US 6 (4mm) needles

NOTIONS
- Pair of US 6 (4mm) needles
- Stitch holder
- Darning needle
- Toy stuffing, beanbag beans, or dried lavender

Using US 6 (4mm) needles and yarn A, cast on 5 sts.

Row 1: knit.

Row 2: inc1, k to last st, inc1. (7 sts)

Change to yarn B.

Repeat these two rows until you have 17 sts, changing color evey two rows and ending with a row 2.

Break off these yarns and leave these 17 sts in holder.

Make one more piece the same, but do not break off yarns on second piece. Continue in two-row stripe pattern, turn and work across 17 sts of this piece, cast on one stitch, then knit across 17 sts on stitch holder. (35 sts)

Knit one row.

Next row: inc1, k to last st, inc1. (37 sts)

Next row: knit one row.

Work last two rows once more, then work in garter stitch for eight rows. (39 sts)

Next row: k2tog, k to last 2 sts, k2tog. (37 sts)

Work 3 rows garter st.

Repeat last 4 rows twice more.
(33 sts)

Next row: k2tog, k to last 2sts,
k2tog. (31 sts)

Next row: knit one row.
Repeat last two rows until
3 sts remain.

Next row: k3tog.
Fasten off yarn.
Make one more piece for the back
using yarn A only.

FINISHING

Sew together two pieces, leaving
small gap in seam for stuffing. Fill
with toy stuffing or chosen filling
to desired fullness. Sew up gap.

Skill Level

Ladybug Lavender Bags

These sweet lavender bags are so cute you may not want to pop them away in your drawers or wardrobe, but leave them near a radiator to freshen the room naturally. You may even wish to stuff them instead with toy stuffing to create a regular toy, or with beanbag granules to make beanbag bugs.

MEASUREMENTS

❷ **Large bug**: approx 4in (10cm) wide

❷ **Small bug**: approx 2½in (6.5cm) wide

SKILL LEVEL

❷ Intermediate

YARN

❷ **Yarn A**: 1 x 1¾oz (50g)—approx 137yd (125m)—Millamia Merino, 100% merino,

Large bug: shade 140 scarlet

Small bug: shade 143 fuchsia

❷ **Yarn B**: 1 x 1¾oz (50g)—approx 131yd (120m)—Rico Essentials Merino DK, 100% merino wool, in shade 90, black

ALTERNATIVE YARNS

❷ This project uses only small amounts of yarn, so you could use scraps of any other DK or sportweight yarn to create the ladybugs

GAUGE (TENSION)

❷ This is not essential but 23 sts to 4in (10cm) in garter stitch using US 5 (3.75mm) needles is good to aim for

NOTIONS

❷ Pair of US 5 (3.75mm) needle

❷ Assorted buttons for eyes and spots

❷ Each bug needs two small circles of fabric to make pouch for the filling, approx 4in (10cm) in diameter for large ladybug and 2in (5cm) in diameter for the small one

❷ Either toy stuffing or a mixture of PVC bean bag granules and lavender to fill

❷ Darning needle

❷ Sewing needle

Large Ladybug (worked in garter stitch)

BELLY

**Using US 5 (3.75mm) needles and yarn A, cast on 5 sts.

Row 1: knit.

Row 2: cast on three stitches, k to end of row. (8 sts)

Row 3: cast on three stitches, k to end of row. (11 sts)

   Work 2 rows straight in garter stitch without increasing.

Row 6: cast on three stitches, k to end of row. (14 sts)

Row 7: cast on three stitches, k to end of row. (17 sts)

   Work 4 rows straight in garter stitch without increasing.

Row 12: cast on two stitches, k to end of row. (19 sts)

Row 13: cast on two stitches, k to end of row. (21 sts)

   Work 5 rows straight in garter stitch without increasing.

Row 19: inc1 at either end of row. (23 sts)

   Work 7 rows straight in garter stitch without increasing.

Row 27: k2tog at either end of row. (21 sts)**

Work 5 rows straight in garter stitch without decreasing.

Row 33: bind (cast) off two stitches, k to end of row. (19 sts)

Row 34: bind (cast) off two stitches, k to end of row. (17 sts)

Work 4 rows straight in garter stitch without decreasing.

Row 39: bind (cast) off three stitches, k to end of row. (14 sts)

Row 40: bind (cast) off three stitches, k to end of row. (11 sts)

Work 2 rows straight in garter stitch without decreasing.

Row 43: bind (cast) off three stitches, k to end of row. (8 sts)

Row 44: bind (cast) off three stitches, k to end of row. (5 sts)

Row 45: knit.

Bind (cast) off all sts.

BACK

Work as for Belly from ** to **.

Change to yarn B and work the rest of the Back same as the Belly in but using yarn B.

Small ladybug (worked in garter stitch)

BELLY

**Using US 5 (3.75mm) needles and yarn A, cast on 3 sts.

Row 1: knit.

Row 2: cast on three stitches, k to end of row. (6 sts)

Row 3: cast on three stitches, k to end of row. (9 sts)

Work 2 rows straight in garter stitch without increasing.

Row 6: cast on two stitches, k to end of row. (11 sts)

Row 7: cast on two stitches, k to end of row. (13 sts)

Work 4 rows straight in garter stitch without increasing.

Row 12: inc one stitch at either end of row. (15 sts)

Work 5 rows straight in garter stitch without increasing.

Row 18: dec one stitch at either end of row. (13 sts)**

Work 4 rows straight in garter stitch without decreasing.

Row 23: bind (cast) off two stitches, k to end of row. (11 sts)

Row 24: bind (cast) off two stitches, k to end of row. (9 sts)

Work 2 rows straight in garter stitch without decreasing.

Row 27: bind (cast) off three stitches, k to end of row. (6 sts)

Row 28: bind (cast) off three stitches, k to end of row. (3 sts)

Row 29: knit.

Bind (cast) off all three stitches.

BACK

Work as for Belly from ** to **.

Change to yarn B and work the rest of the Back same as the Belly in but using yarn B.

FINISHING

If using lavender/beanbag granules:

Sew together two circles of fabric, around edge, leaving a small gap of about ½in (1cm).

Turn pouch inside out and, using a funnel, fill with the lavender and/or beanbag granules to desired fullness.

Sew up gap.

Place pouch on Belly piece, then lay the Back on top of it and sew together knitted pieces all round edge, using darning needle and yarn A, trapping the pouch.

IF USING TOY STUFFING:

Sew together Belly and Back pieces all round edge using darning needle and yarn A, leaving a gap of about ½in (1cm). Stuff bug with toy stuffing through this opening, then sew up gap.

Skill Level

Rainbow Pillow

If you want a fun and easy way to learn how to shape your knitting, look no further than this simple pattern. Each zigzagged stripe is a single strip of knitting that is worked by simply increasing and decreasing.

MEASUREMENTS
- ❶ One size, finished cushion is approx 12 x 12in (30 x 30cm)

SKILL LEVEL
- ❶ Intermediate

YARN
- ❶ 1 x 1¾oz (50g)—approx 127yd (116m)—of Sublime Cashmere Merino Silk DK, 75% extra fine merino, 20% silk, 5% cashmere, in each of:
- ❶ **Yarn A:** shade 119 lido
- ❶ **Yarn B:** shade 124 splash
- ❶ **Yarn C:** shade 194 seesaw
- ❶ **Yarn D:** shade 195 puzzle

- ❶ **Yarn E:** shade 122 honeybunny
- ❶ **Yarn F:** shade 158 ladybug
- ❶ **Yarn G:** shade td53 purple

ALTERNATIVE YARNS
- ❶ Any DK or sportweight yarn will achieve the same size cushion, although you could use any weight of yarn and the cushion will simply come out a different size, so you will have to hold off buying the cushion pad until it is finished. Always buy a cushion pad slightly larger than your piece of fabric, so that the fabric stretches over it—there is nothing worse than a floppy cushion!

GAUGE (TENSION)
- ❶ 22 sts and 28 rows to 4in (10cm) in stockinette (stocking) stitch using US 6 (4mm) needles

NOTIONS
- ❶ Pair of US 6 (4mm) needles
- ❶ Darning needle
- ❶ 12 x 12in (30 x 30cm) cushion pad

STRIP 1

Using US 6 (4mm) needles and yarn A, cast on 6 sts.

Row 1 (RS): knit.

Row 2: purl.

**Row 3: k2, inc1, k to last two sts, inc1, k2.

Row 4: purl.

Repeat rows 3–4 until you have 16 sts, ending with a purl row.

Next row: k2, k2tog, k to last four sts, k2tog, k2.

Next row: purl.

Repeat last two rows until you have 6 sts, ending with a purl row.**

Repeat from ** to ** eight more times, so you have nine full repeats.

Bind (cast) off all sts.

Make three more strips, one in each of yarns C, E, and G.

STRIP 2

Using US 6 (4mm) needles, and yarn B, cast on 16 sts.

Row 1 (RS): knit.

Row 2: purl.

**Row 3: k2, k2tog, k to last four sts, k2tog, k2.

Row 4: purl.

Repeat rows 3–4 until you have 6 sts, ending with a purl row.

Next row: k2, inc1, k to last two sts, inc1, k2.

Next row: purl.

Repeat last two rows until you have 16 sts, ending with a purl row.**

Repeat from ** to ** eight more times, so you have nine full repeats.

Bind (cast) off all sts.

Make two more strips, one in each of yarns D and F.

FINISHING

Lay out all strips in alphabetical order A to G and with the right side facing down. Sew all strips together on the back with whip stitch, so that the zigzags fit together and the top and bottom are straight.

Fold around a cushion pad and sew up the three side seams.

Playtime

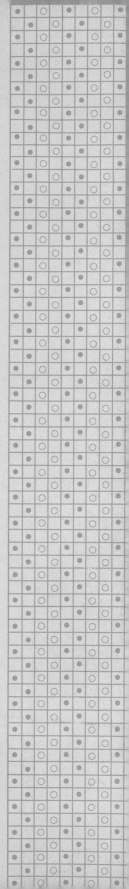

- Doctor's stethoscope
- Stripey ball
- Candy bonbons
- Cakes and treats
- Sheriff's badge
- Teddy bear
- Beard and moustache
- Alien
- Rag doll

Skill Level

Doctor's Stethoscope

Make yourself a French-knitted stethoscope for dressing up as a doctor and check that all your toys are in the best of health!

MEASUREMENTS
- ❶ One size

SKILL LEVEL
- ❶ Intermediate

YARN
- ❶ 1 x 1¾oz (50g)—approx 127yd (116m)—of Sublime Cashmere Merino Silk DK, 75% extra fine merino, 20% silk, 5% cashmere, in shade td53 purple

YARN ALTERNATIVES
- ❶ Any yarn will do, but a DK weight will create the

same size tubes as here. Try inserting pipe cleaners into the tube to bend the stethoscope into shapes

GAUGE (TENSION)
- ❶ Not necessary

NOTIONS
- ❶ French knitting bobbin
- ❶ Darning needle
- ❶ Large button

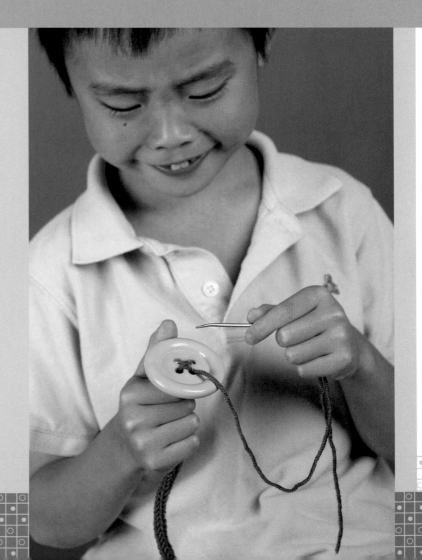

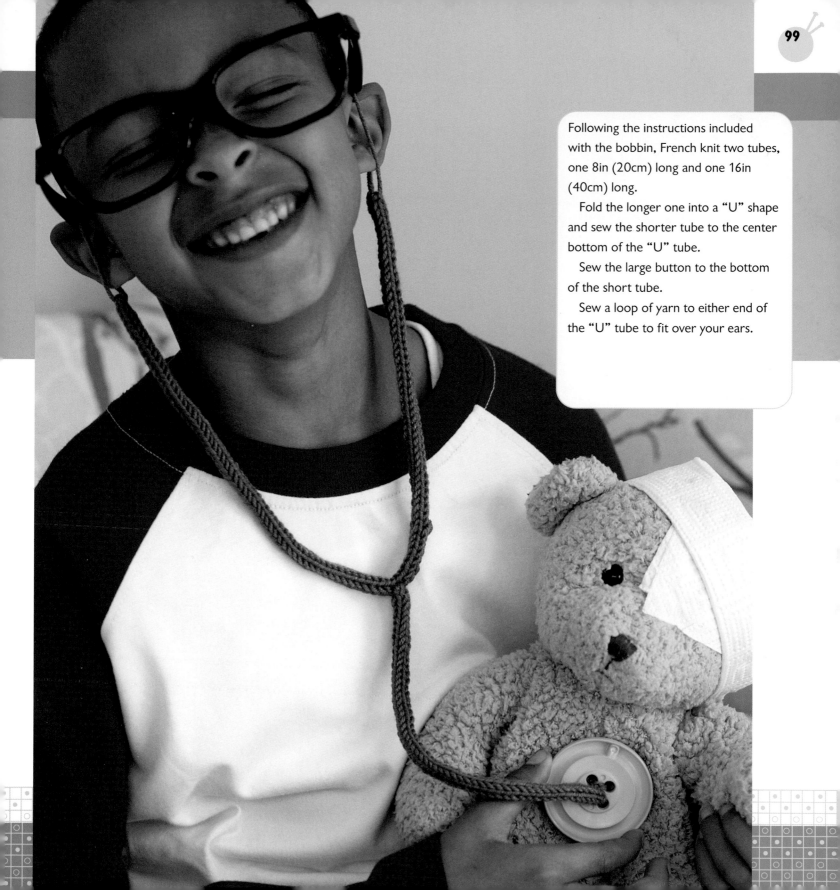

Following the instructions included with the bobbin, French knit two tubes, one 8in (20cm) long and one 16in (40cm) long.

Fold the longer one into a "U" shape and sew the shorter tube to the center bottom of the "U" tube.

Sew the large button to the bottom of the short tube.

Sew a loop of yarn to either end of the "U" tube to fit over your ears.

Stripey Ball

Hours of fun can be had with this easy-to-make ball. Make three and learn to juggle with them, make up a throwing and catching game, or see who can throw them the furthest (outdoors, of course!). You can stuff them with toy stuffing, or for more weight when juggling, fill with beans or beanbag granules.

MEASUREMENTS

❂ One size, approx 12in (30cm) around widest part

SKILL LEVEL

❂ Intermediate

YARN

❂ 1 x 1¾oz (50g)—approx 137yd (125m)—Millamia Merino, 100% merino, in each of:
❂ **Yarn A:** shade 140 scarlet
❂ **Yarn B:** shade 141 grass
❂ **Yarn C:** shade 144 peacock

YARN ALTERNATIVES

❂ Any DK weight yarn will do here to create balls of the same dimensions a these, but use thicker yarn if you want a more football-shaped ball, or thinner yarn for smaller juggling balls

GAUGE (TENSION)

❂ 22 sts and 30 rows to 4in (10cm) in stockinette (stocking) stitch using US 5 (3.75mm) needles

NOTIONS

❂ Pair of US 5 (3.75mm) needles
❂ Darning needle
❂ Toy stuffing or beanbag granules

Using US 5 (3.75mm) needles and yarn A, cast on 3 sts.

Row 1: inc1, k1, inc1. (5 sts)

Row 2: purl.

Row 3: inc1, k to last st, inc1. (7 sts)

Row 4: purl.

Row 5: inc1, k to last st, inc1. (9 sts)

Work 3 rows st st.

Row 9: inc1, k to last st, inc1. (11 sts)

Work 5 rows st st.

Row 15: inc1, k to last st, inc1. (13 sts)

Work 15 rows st st.

Row 31: k2tog, k to last 2 sts, k2tog. (11 sts)

Work 5 rows st st.

Row 37: k2tog, k to last 2 sts, k2tog. (9 sts)

Work 3 rows st st.

Row 41: k2tog, k to last 2 sts, k2tog. (7 sts)

Row 42: purl.

Row 43: k2tog, k to last 2 sts, k2tog. (5 sts)

Row 44: purl.
Row 45: k2tog, k1, k2tog. (3 sts)
  Bind (cast) off all sts.

Make one more segment in yarn A and 2 segments in each of
yarns B and C: six segments in total.
  Sew all six segments together, with no colors the same next
to each other, all along the long sides, leaving the last seam
half sewn. Fill ball with toy stuffing and/or beans to desired
fullness and sew up gap.

Skill Level

Candy Bonbons

These sweet treats will look delicious piled up in a bowl in your bedroom and will make cute gifts for your friends.

MEASUREMENTS

❶ One size, each sweet is approx 3¼in (8cm) from side to side

YARN

❶ 1 x 1¾oz (50g)—approx 137yd (125m)—Millamia Merino, 100% merino, in each of:

❶ **Yarn A**: shade 141 grass

❶ **Yarn B**: shade 143 fuchsia

❶ **Yarn C**: shade 144 peacock

❶ 1 x 1¾oz (50g)—approx 131yd (120m)—Rico Essentials Merino DK, 100% merino wool, in:

❶ **Yarn D**: shade 64 lime

YARN ALTERNATIVES

❶ Any DK weight yarn will do, but a specific gauge (tension) is not essential. You could try any yarn and the sweets will just come out different sizes. You could also try some metallic yarns for sparkle, or stripe up the colors for different patterns.

GAUGE (TENSION)

❶ 22 sts and 28 rows to 4in (10cm) in stockinette (stocking) stitch using US 6 (4mm) needles

NOTIONS

❶ Pair of US 6 (4mm) needles

❶ Darning needle

❶ Sewing needle and thread

❶ Toy stuffing

❶ Assorted narrow ribbons for decoration

Using US 6 (4mm) needles and choice of yarn color, cast on 29 sts.

Row 1 (RS): knit.

Row 2: purl.

Rep rows 1–2 twice more.

Row 7: k1, [yo, k2tog] to end of row.

Work 7 rows st st, beginning with a purl row.

Next row: k1, [k2tog] to end of row. (15 sts)

Work 9 rows st st, beginning with a purl row.

Next row: k1, [inc1] to end of row. (29 sts)

Work 7 rows st st, beginning with a purl row.

Next row: k1, [yo, k2tog] to end of row.

Work 6 rows st st, beginning with a purl row.

Bind off (cast off) all sts.

FINISHING

Fold back one end of strip along row of holes (this line will want to fold automatically), and sew into place to make a scallopped hem. Do the same with opposite end.

Sew up side seam of sweet.

Using a darning needle. thread a length of yarn in and out of the stitches along the line of one hem, pull tight and tie to secure. Stuff the middle of the sweet with toy stuffing, then thread another length of yarn in and out of the stitches along the line of the other hem and pull tight to trap toy stuffing in.

Tie ribbon into small bows around each gathered end.

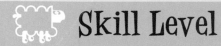

Skill Level
Cakes and Treats

Knitting that is good enough to eat—almost! Fool your friends with fake food, have a dolls' tea party, or use the cakes as pincushions

MEASUREMENTS

One size

❶ **Donut** approx 4in (10cm) in diameter

❶ **Sponge** approx 2¾in (7cm) diameter

❶ **Cupcake** approx 2¾in (7cm) diameter

SKILL LEVEL

❶ Easy

YARN

Cakes

❶ 1 x 1¾oz (50g)—approx 137yd (125m)—Millamia Merino, 100% merino, in each of:

❶ **Yarn A**: shade 160 fawn

❶ **Yarn B**: shade 143 fuchsia

❶ **Yarn C**: shade 162 plum

❶ **Yarn D**: shade 123 lilac blossom

❶ 1 x 1¾oz (50g)—approx 131yd (120m)—Rico Essentials Merino DK, 100% merino wool, in:

❶ **Yarn E**: shade 10 magenta

YARN ALTERNATIVES

❶ Any DK weight yarn will do here, but as a specific gauge (tension) is not essential you could try any yarn and the cakes will just come out different sizes.

GAUGE (TENSION)

❶ 25 sts and 32 rows to 4in (10cm) in stockinette (stocking) stitch using US 5 (3.75mm) needles

NOTIONS

❶ Pair each of US 5 (3.75mm) needles

❶ Darning needle

❶ Sewing needle and thread

❶ Cardboard

❶ Beads and buttons for decoration

❶ Toy stuffing

❶ Felt

❶ French knitting doll

Donut

Using US 5 (3.75mm) needles and yarn A, cast on 50 sts.

Row 1(RS): knit.

Row 2: purl.

Rep last two rows until work measures approx 2¾in (7cm).

Change to yarn E and work in st st as before for 2in (5cm).

Bind (cast) off all sts.

FINISHING

Sew cast on edge to bound (cast) off edge and stuff resulting tube to desired fullness with toy stuffing.

Sew tube into donut shape by joining side seams together.

Decorate with bugle beads to represent sprinkles.

Sponge

Using US 5 (3.75mm) needles and yarn A, cast on 40 sts.

Row 1(RS): purl.

Row 2: knit.

Work approx 2¾in (7cm) in yarn A in reverse st st as set.

Change to yarn B and work two rows reverse st st for jam filling.

Change back to A and cont in reverse st st for 2¾in (7cm).

Cut yarn but do not bind (cast) off. Thread tail through rem sts and pull up tight to gather. Secure, then sew up side seam. Insert a small circle of cardboard of approx 2¼in (6cm) in diameter to form a base then stuff the rest of cake with toy stuffing to desired fullness. Insert another circle of approx 2¼in (6cm) diameter on top of the stuffing. Using matching sewing thread, work a row of running stitches around cast-on edge and pull up to gather at top. Sew firmly closed. Sew a large red glass bead to top of sponge, over gathered center, for a cherry.

Cupcake

Using US 5 (3.75mm) needles, and yarn B, cast on 12 sts.

Row 1(RS): knit.

Row 2: purl.

Change to yarn C and work two rows st st as set.

Cont in st st working 2 rows of each color alternately until work measures approx 8in (20cm).

Bind (cast) off all sts.

Using yarn D, French-knit a length of tube approx 20in (51cm) long.

Cut a circle of felt of approx 2¼in (6cm) in diameter.

Sew cast on edge of long strip to bound-(cast-) off edge. Sew this ring to the felt circle, around the circumference.

Stuff this striped section with toy stuffing to desired fullness.

Begin to sew the French knitted tube to the top of the striped section all around the edge, winding it around on itself to create a spiral of French-knitted tube. Leave a gap unsewn at top and stuff the cone of French-knitted icing. Sew up gap.

Decorate with small round beads for sprinkles and add a large glass bead on top for a cherry, if desired.

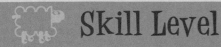

Skill Level

Sheriff's Badge

Every town needs a sheriff to keep an eye on things, so knit yourself a star and pin it to your chest, wear it with a cowboy hat and chase the bank robbers outta town!

MEASUREMENTS

❷ One size, approx 4in (10cm) in diameter

SKILL LEVEL

❷ Easy

YARN

❷ 1 x 1¾oz (50g)—approx 137yd (125m)—Millamia Merino, 100% merino, in shade 142 daisy yellow
❷ Scraps of yarn for embroidery

YARN ALTERNATIVES

❷ Any DK weight yarn will do here as gauge (tension) is not essential. You could try any yarn and the star will just come out different sizes. You could also try some metallic yarns to make it look like a real metal star

GAUGE (TENSION)

❷ 24 sts and 30 rows to 4in (10cm) in stockinette (stocking) stitch using US 5 (3.75mm) needles

NOTIONS

❷ Pair of US 5 (3.75mm) needles
❷ Darning needle
❷ Toy stuffing
❷ Sewing needle and thread
❷ Safety pin or brooch back

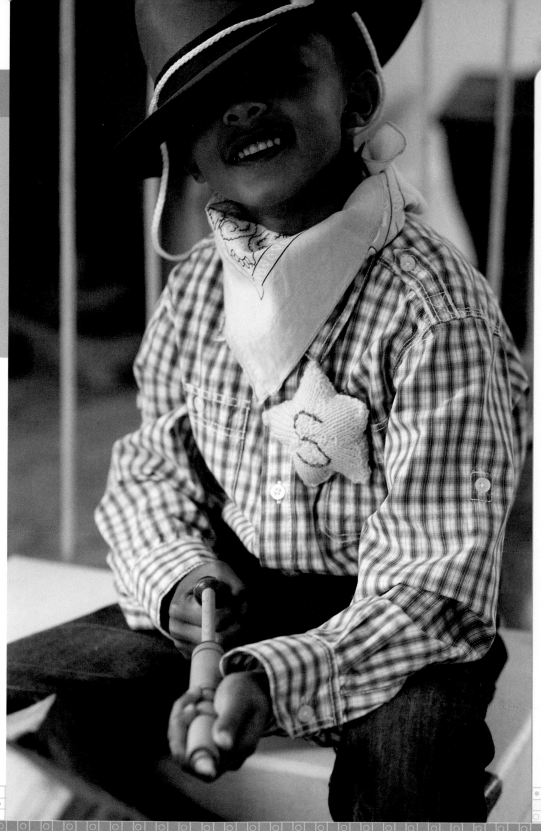

Using US 5 (3.75mm) needles, cast on 3 sts.

Next row: inc1, k to last st, inc1.

Next row: purl.

Rep last two rows until there are 11 sts, ending with a p row.

Next row: k2tog, k to last 2 sts, k2tog.

Next row: purl.

Rep last two rows until 3 sts rem, ending with a p row.

Next row: k3tog.

Fasten off yarn.

Make 9 more pieces the same, 10 pieces in total.

Sew 5 pieces together in a circle, butting the lower sides of the diamond-shapes together. Do the same with the other 5 pieces.

Wrong sides facing, sew the two stars together leaving a small gap.

Stuff star with toy stuffing to desired fullness.

Sew up gap.

Using contrast yarn, embroider an "S" onto front of star with simple straight stitches.

Sew brooch back to back of star.

Skill Level

Teddy Bear

Everyone has a favorite toy and this cute teddy is bound to become yours with his smiley little face and squishy body.

MEASUREMENTS

❶ One size, approz 11in (28cm) high

SKILL LEVEL

❷ Intermediate

YARN

❸ 1 x 1¾oz (50g)—approx 137yd (125m)—of Regia Softy, 39% new wool, 61% polyamide, in shade 435 beige

ALTERNATIVE YARNS

❹ Any DK or sportweight yarn will achieve the same size teddy, but you could try other weights and your teddy will just come out bigger or smaller. Here, the yarn is a furry, textured yarn that is incredibly soft and cozy, but you could experiment with other textures, although using a machine washable yarn is a good idea so that when you have played with and hugged teddy so much that he is grubby, it is easy to make him as good as new.

GAUGE (TENSION)

❺ 24 sts and 32 rows to 4in (10cm) in stockinette (stocking) stitch using US 6 (4mm) needles

NOTIONS

❻ Pair of US 6 (4mm) needles

❼ Darning needle

❽ Toy stuffing

❾ Buttons for eyes

❿ Ribbon for decoration, if desired

⓫ Oddments of embroidery thread or yarn for face

Note: you can use either side of the st st as the right side on this pattern, or a mixture of both, as here, to use both textures—each looks good in this furry yarn.

LEGS

Using US 6 (4mm) needles, cast on 20 sts and work 4¼in (11cm) in st st.

Do not bind (cast) off.

Break yarn and thread through rem sts, pulling up tight. Sew side seam to form a tube and stuff leg with toy stuffing to desired fullness.

Thread yarn in and out all around cast-on edge of leg and pull up tight to close.

ARMS

Using US 6 (4mm) needles, cast on
16 sts and work 3¼in (8cm) in st st
   Do not bind (cast) off.
   Break yarn and thread through rem
sts, pulling up tight. Sew side seam
and stuff arm with toy stuffing to
desired fullness.
   Thread yarn in and out all around
cast-on edge of arm and pull up tight
to close.

BODY

Using US 6 (4mm) needles, cast on
50 sts and work 4¼in (11cm) in st st.
   Do not bind (cast) off.
   Break yarn and thread through rem
sts, pulling up tight. Sew side seam
and stuff body with toy stuffing to
desired fullness.
   Thread yarn in and out all around
cast-on edge of body and pull up tight
to close.

HEAD

Using US 6 (4mm) needles, cast on 60 sts and work 3½in (9cm) in st st.

Do not bind (cast) off.

Break yarn and thread through rem sts, pulling up tight. Sew side seam and stuff head with toy stuffing to desired fullness.

Thread yarn in and out all around cast-on edge of head and pull up tight to close.

EARS

Using US 6 (4mm) needles, cast on 9 sts.

Knit one row.

Next row: k2tog, k to last 2 sts, k2tog.

Rep last two rows until 5 sts rem.

Knit one row.

Bind (cast) off all sts.

FINISHING

Sew head and limbs to body.

Sew ears to head, along with buttons for eyes and embroider on a mouth and nose.

Tie ribbon around teddy's neck, if desired.

Skill Level

Beard and Moustache

These fake facial hairpieces are the perfect disguise for playing at being a spy, or for fancy dress! You do not have to stick to natural hair colors—try mad brights!

MEASUREMENTS

❷ One size

SKILL LEVEL

❷ Intermediate

YARN

Beard

❷ 1 x 1¾oz (50g)—approx 169yd (155m)—of Regia Pompon 43% wool, 37% polyamide, 18% polyester, in shade 275

Moustache

❷ 1 x 1¾oz (50g)—approx 114yd (105m)—of Wendy Allegra, 32% Alpaca, 31% acrylic, 37% polyester, in shade 957

GAUGE (TENSION)

❷ Not necessary

NOTIONS

❷ Pair each of US 10 (6mm) and US 4 (3.5mm) needles

❷ Darning needle

Beard

Using US 4 (3.5mm) needles, cast on 20 sts.

Working in garter st (every row knit), inc1 at start of every other row until you have 26 sts.

Work straight in garter st for 1¼in (3cm), ending at straight side.

Next row: k5, bind (cast) off two sts for mouth, k to end.

Work in garter stitch on these 19 sts for 1¼in (3cm), ending at mouth edge.

Rejoin yarn to 5 unworked sts and work in garter st on these 5 sts until piece measures same as worked side of mouth, ending at mouth edge.

Cast on 2 sts over mouth, k to end of row. (26 sts).

Work straight on these sts for 1¼in (3cm) ending at straight side, then k2tog at end of next and every other row until 20 sts rem.

Bind (cast) off all sts.

Finger-knit two lengths of chain of approx 20in (51cm) and attach one to either side of top edge of beard to tie beard on.

Moustache

Using US 10 (6mm) needles, cast on 12 sts.

Working in garter st (every row knit), inc1 at either end of next 2 rows. (16 sts)

Cast on 8 sts at end of next row.

Bind (cast) off these same 8 sts at beg of next row and cast on 8 more at the end of next row.

Bind (cast) off all sts.

Finger-knit two lengths of chain (see page 41) approx 20in (50cm) long and attach one to either thick side of moustache to tie moustache on.

Roll thin ends of moustache up and allow to sit twisted as with a real "curled-at-the-ends" moustache.

Skill Level

Alien

Cute and weird alien toys made out of fur yarn can be embellished in many ways to create unique little critters.

MEASUREMENTS

❷ One size, approx 8in (20cm) tall

SKILL LEVEL

❸ Intermediate

YARN

❷ **Yarn A**: 1 x 1¾oz (50g)—approx 71yd (65m)—Sirdar Escape Wool Rich Chunky, 51% wool, 49% acrylic, in shade 197

❷ **Yarn B**: 1 x 1¾oz (50g)—approx 43yd (40m)—Gedifra Antiga, 34% acrylic, 30% polyamide, 18% mohair, 18% wool, in shade 3101

ALTERNATIVE YARNS

❷ Any bulky weight yarn can be used to replicate this alien; as gauge (tension) is not important, the toy will just vary in size. You could also try knitting it all in a fur yarn, or all in a regular yarn

GAUGE (TENSION)

❷ 10 sts and 14 rows to 4in (10cm) in garter stitch using US 11 (8mm) needles

NOTIONS

❷ Pair of US 11 (8mm) needles
❷ Darning needle
❷ Toy stuffing
❷ Buttons for eyes
❷ Felt for limbs

Using yarn A and US 11 (8mm) needles, cast on 12 sts.

Row 1: knit.

Row 2: inc1, k to last st, inc1. (14 sts)

Rep last 2 rows until you have 22 sts.

Work straight in garter st until work measures 3¼in (8cm) from cast on edge.

Change to yarn B and work 2in (5cm) in garter st.

Next row: k2tog, k to last 2 sts, k2tog. (20 sts)

Next row: knit.

Rep last 2 rows once more. (18 sts)

Cont on these 18 sts for 1¼in (3cm).

Next row: k4, turn, leaving rem sts unworked.

Work 4 rows garter st on these 4 sts.

Next row: [k2tog] twice. (2 sts)

Next row: knit.

Next row: k2tog, fasten off yarn.

Rejoin yarn to rem 14 sts, k5, turn, leaving rem sts unworked.

Work 4 rows garter st on these 5 sts.

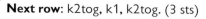

Next row: k2tog, k1, k2tog. (3 sts)

Next row: knit.

Next row: k3tog, fasten off yarn.

Rejoin yarn to rem 9 sts, k5, turn, leaving rem sts unworked.

Work 4 rows garter st on these 5 sts.

Next row: k2tog, k1, k2tog. (3 sts)

Next row: knit.

Next row: k3tog, fasten off yarn.

Rejoin yarn to rem 4 sts, k4.

Work 4 further rows garter st on these 4 sts.

Next row: [k2tog] twice. (2 sts)

Next row: knit.

Next row: k2tog, fasten off yarn.

Make one more piece in the same way.

FINISHING

Cut out four felt triangles for arms and four slightly larger felt triangles for legs.

Sew the arm pieces together, leaving one seam open for stuffing. Fill with toy stuffing to desired fullness and sew up gap.

Sew two body pieces together, inserting the arms and legs in position and sewing in place as you go. Leave a small gap for stuffing.

Fill with toy stuffing to desired fullness and sew up gap.

Attach eyes to the yarn A section of alien. You can also embroider a mouth and any other weird or scary features you want.

Rag Doll

It is easy to make your little rag doll different from everyone else's by changing her hair color—perhaps to match your own or even a fun, bright shade. You can sew on different features for her face or add sewn fabric clothes or pockets. Have fun!

MEASUREMENTS

- One size, approx 23in (58.5cm) tall

SKILL LEVEL

- Difficult

YARN

- 1 x 1¾oz (50g)—approx 84yd (77m)—Mission Falls 1824 cotton, 100% cotton, in each of:
- **Yarn A**: shade 200 biscuit
- **Yarn B**: shade 407 aubergine
- **Yarn C**: shade 202 cardinal
- **Yarn D**: shade 302 green

GAUGE (TENSION)

- 18 sts and 24 rows to 4in (10cm) in stockinette (stocking) stitch using US 7 (4.5mm) needles

NOTIONS

- Pair of US 7 (4.5mm) needles
- Darning needle
- Toy stuffing
- Scraps of felt for cheeks
- Sewing needle and thread
- Buttons for eyes and for dress

BODY

Using US 7 (4.5mm) needles and yarn A, cast on 40 sts.

Work 5½in (14cm) in st st.

Bind (cast) off all sts.

Fold piece in half widthways and sew up two of the seams. Fill the body with toy stuffing to desired fullness then sew up the remaining seam.

HEAD

Using US 7 (4.5mm) needles and yarn A, cast on 12 sts.

Row 1: knit.

Row 2: purl.

Row 3: inc1, k to last st, inc1. (14 sts)

Row 4: purl.

Rep last two rows until you have 24 sts, ending with a row 4

Cont in st st without increasing for 8 rows, ending with a p row.

Next row: k2tog, k to last 2 sts, k2tog. (22 sts)

Next row: purl.

Rep last two rows until you have 12 sts.

Bind (cast) off all sts.

Make one more piece the same, but using yarn B.

Sew two pieces together all round edge, with yarn B piece as back of head with purl side as right side and yarn A piece as face with knit side as right side. Leave a small gap for stuffing. Fill with toy stuffing to desired fullness and sew up gap.

ARMS (MAKE TWO)

Using US 7 (4.5mm) needles and yarn A, cast on 6 sts.

Work 5½in (14cm) in st st.

Bind (cast) off all sts.

Fold piece in half widthways and sew up one short seam and the long seam. Fill the arm with toy stuffing to desired fullness then sew up the remaining short seam.

LEGS (MAKE TWO)

Using US 7 (4.5mm) needles and yarn B, cast on 11 sts.

Work in st st for two rows.

Change to yarn C and work 2 rows st st.

Cont straight in st st in this way, working stripes as established until legs measure 12in (30cm).

Bind (cast) off all sts.

Fold piece in half widthways and sew up one short seam and the long seam. Fill the leg with toy stuffing to desired fullness then sew up the remaining short seam.

BODY FINISHING

Sew head, arms, and legs to body, with arms approx ½in (1cm) down from the top of body and legs attached to bottom seam of body.

DRESS

Using US 7 (4.5mm) needles and yarn D, cast on 28 sts.

Working in st st, k2tog at either end of 7th and every foll 8th row until 20 sts remain.

Cont straight until work measures 6¼in (16cm).

Bind (cast) off all sts.

Make one more piece the same.

Sew dress pieces together, around the body, leaving holes in the side seams for the arms and in center of top seam for head.

POCKET

Using US 7 (4.5mm) needles and yarn C, cast on 9 sts.

Row 1: purl.

Row 2: inc1, k to last st, inc1. (11 sts)

Rep last two rows once more. (13 sts)

Work 5 rows st st.

Bind (cast) off all sts.

Sew to dress front using yarn B. Sew on buttons.

HAIR PLAITS

Cut 12 lengths of yarn B 49in (124cm) long. Keeping the strands in a bunch, safety pin the mid point to the center of your doll's head. Using yarn C, attach the tassel by sewing around the hair at the top corners of your doll's head. Remove the safety pin. Spilt one side of the tassel's 12 ends into 3 sections (4 strands each section) and plait to the end, tying a knot at the bottom to secure. Repeat for the other side.

FINISHING

Sew on button eyes. Cur circles of felt and sew them on for cheeks. Embroider other features in yarn.

Abbreviations

alt	alternate		**p2tog**	purl two stitches together
beg	beginning		**patt**	pattern
cont	continue		**rem**	remaining
dec	decrease		**rep**	repeat
DK	double knitting (yarn weight)		**rev st st**	reverse stockinette (stocking) stitch
foll(s)	follow(s) (ing)			
inc1	increase		**RS**	right side
k	knit		**st(s)**	stitch(es)
k2tog	knit two stitches together		**st st**	stockinette (stocking) stitch
k3tog	knit three stitches together		**tog**	together
p	purl		**WS**	wrong side

Suppliers

USA

DEBBIE BLISS
SIRDAR
SUBLIME
Knitting Fever Inc.
PO Box 336
315 Bayview Ave
Amityville
NY 11701
Tel: 516-546-3600
Fax: 516-546-6871

ROWAN YARNS
REGIA
Westminster Fibers Inc.
4 Townsend West
Suite 8
Nashua
NH 03063
Tel: 063-886-5041
www.westminsterfibers.com

PATONS
Coats & Clark
Consumer Services
P.O. Box 12229
Greenville
SC 29612-0229
Tel: 800-648-1479
www.coatsandclark.com

MISSION FALLS
CNS Yarns c/o Milgram
156 Lawrence Paquette
Champlain
NY 12919
info@missionfalls.com

PURL (SHOP)
459 Broome Street
New York
NY 10013
Tel: 212-420-8796
www.purlsoho.com

DOWNTOWN YARNS
(SHOP)
45 Avenue A
New York
NY 10009
Tel: 212-995-5991
www.downtownyarns.com

Canada

PATONS
320 Livingstone Avenue South
Listowel
Ontario N4W 3H3
Tel: 1-888-368-8401
www.patonsyarns.com

DEBBIE BLISS
REGIA
ROWAN YARNS
SIRDAR
SUBLIME
Diamond Yarns Ltd
155 Martin Ross Avenue
Unit 3
Toronto
Ontario M3J 2L9
Tel: 416-736-6111
www.diamondyarn.com

MISSION FALLS
Head office Canada
5333 Casgrain 1204
Montreal
Quebec
H2T 1X3
Tel: 1-877-244-1204
Fax: 514-279-3885
info@missionfalls.com

UK

SIRDAR SPINNING LTD.
Flanshaw Lane
Wakefield
West Yorkshire WF2 9ND
United Kingdom
Tel: 01924 231669
Email: orders@sirdar.co.uk

MISSION FALLS
Hantex Ltd
Unit 1 Whitehouse Business Units
Eaudyke
Friskney
Lincolnshire PE22 8NL
Tel: 01754 820800
Fax: 01754 820110
www.hantex.co.uk

DEBBIE BLISS
Designer Yarns
Unit 8-10 Newbridge Industrial
Estate
Pitt Street
Keighley
West Yorkshire BD21 4PQ
Tel: 01535 664222
Fax: 01535 664333
www.designeryarns.uk.com

ROWAN YARNS
Green Lane Mill
Holmfirth
West Yorkshire HD9 2DX
Tel: 01484 681881
www.knitrowan.com

PATONS
Coats Crafts UK
PO Box 22
Lingfield House
Lingfield Point
McMullen Road
Darlington
County Durham DL1 1YQ
Tel: 01325 394237
www.coatscrafts.co.uk

MILLAMIA
Tel: 08450 177474.
www.millamia.com

MRS MOON (SHOP)
41 Crown Road
St Margarets
Twickenham
Middlesex TW1 3EJ
Tel: 020 8744 1190
www.mrsmoon.co.uk

LOOP (SHOP)
15 Camden Passage
Islington
London N1 8EA
Tel: 020 7288 1160
Email: info@loopknitting.com

GET KNITTED (SHOP)
39 Brislington Hill
Brislington
Bristol BS4 5BE
Tel: 0117 3005211
www.getknitted.com

International

RICO YARNS
RICO DESIGN GmbH & Co.
KG Industriestrasse 19 - 23
33034 Brakel
Germany

BC GARN
BC Garn Aps,
Elbow 56A
DK – 6000 Kolding
Denmark
+45 75 89 73 84
www.bcgarn.dk

Acknowledgments

This has been an incredibly fun book to write, knit, and shoot and it would not have been half so much fun if it wasn't for some of the people who have helped it into being.

Firstly I must thank the models: Emilie, Reo, Alice, Jocasta, Jemima, Henry, Freddie, Billie, Tilly, Kiera, and Aiden. who were a joy to shoot and, in many cases, had us roaring with laughter, making it feel like anything but work. I cannot forget the contribution of their parents, including Mel, Marcelle, Karen, and Ling, who often patiently knitted away while we were shooting. It has been so lovely to meet so many people who are still passing the love of knitting down to their children, which is what this book is essentially about.

The team who have worked on the book have been fabulous—thanks to Martin, Terry, and Ian the photographers, who have captured the pure joy of knitting with children delightfully. Also thanks to Cindy, Pete, Sally, Elizabeth, Marilyn, and especially Kate for their support and for seeing the book's potential and allowing me realize a dream by finally publishing **Knitting for Children** and making it look so beautiful.

I am extremely grateful to all the yarn companies who donated yarn, especially to the lovely ladies at Millamia and Sublime, who are always incredibly supportive.

My undying gratitude must go to my hardworking mother, Mary, and grandmother, Patsy, and also to my friend, Clare, who have helped out with additional knitting when it all became too much for my hands to cope with.

Finally, to Sean and my family, thanks as always. They have been a fantastic support throughout the many ups and downs of writing a book, meeting deadlines, dealing with AWOL yarn and repetitive strain injuries!

Thank you to you all,

Claire

Index

Toys and Games

Jane Bidder

W
FRANKLIN WATTS
LONDON • SYDNEY

First published in 2006 by
Franklin Watts

Franklin Watts
338 Euston Road
London NW1 3BH

Franklin Watts Australia
Level 17/207 Kent Street
Sydney, NSW 2000

Series editor: Jennifer Schofield
Designer: Ross George
Picture researcher: Diana Morris
Artwork: Ray Bryant
Photography: Ray Moller unless otherwise acknowledged

Acknowledgements:
With special thanks to Mattel Inc for supplying
Polly Pocket and Matchbox and Hot Wheels cars.

The author would like to thank Mary Bellis
of http://inventors.about.com for her help in researching this book.

Antikensammlung, Staatliche Museen, Berlin/Bildarchiv Preussischer Kulturbesitz: 12b;
Sarah Fabian-Baddiel/HIP/Topfoto: 21; The British Library, London: 5br, 10b; British Pathé/
ITN Stills: 19t; Sally Chappel/V & A Museum, London/Art Archive: 16bl. Christies Images:
front cover tl; The Computer History Museum, Ca, USA: 24b; Duncan Toys: 13b; Mary Evans
Picture Library: 22b, 26t; Malcolm Case-Green/Alamy: 24t; Keystone/Topfoto: 25; The National
Yo Yo Museum & Contest, Ca, USA. All rights reserved: 12t; Nicholas Sapieha, Poggio Petroio
Dog Collection/Art Archive: 3br, 10t; Sothebys/AKG Images: 7tr; Tamiya/The Hobby Company
2005; www.tamiya.com: 19b; Michael Teller/AKG Images: 20b; Yves Tzaud/Photographers
Direct: 23; John Warren/Topfoto: 8b; Karl Weatherly/ Corbis: 22t; Jerome Yeats/Alamy: 18.

A CIP catalogue record for this book
is available from the British Library.

ISBN: 978 0 7496 6401 5
Dewey Classification: 790.1'33

Printed in China

Franklin Watts is a division of Hachette Children's Books

Contents

About inventions

An invention is a device or a gadget that is designed and made for the first time. The person who makes the device is called an inventor. In this book, we look at some of the playful inventions that keep us entertained. We will also investigate who invented them and how they have changed over time.

Making life fun

Many toys and games have been invented to help people to relax. The game of chess has been played around the world since 700 CE. Although chess is a game of tactics and you have to concentrate to play it, it is an enjoyable way to spend time with a friend.

From one comes another

Many inventions change and develop from earlier ideas or are improved over time. For example, in 100 CE yo-yos were made from terracotta, which is a heavy clay. Then, much later, in 1400 CE wooden yo-yos were made. Today, most yo-yos are made from plastic. Some even have lights that glow as the yo-yos move up and down.

Learning through play

Many toys were invented to teach children about the adult world, or to help with their education. Map puzzles teach children geography while many board games really make you think! Some toys help you to make up stories in your head. Until the last 200 years, most toys were made from materials found easily around the house.

You will find timelines throughout this book. They show in date order when a specific breakthrough or invention occurred.

Sometimes the dates are very exact, but other times they point to a particular historical era or decade, for example the 1990s.

Use these timelines to keep track of when things happened.

Teddy bears

Teddy bears have not changed much since they were first made over 100 years ago. Today, these cuddly toys are still popular with both adults and children.

Going hunting

In 1902, Theodore (Teddy) Roosevelt, the US President, went hunting. When he refused to shoot a bear cub, the story appeared in a newspaper, showing a cartoon of the president sparing the cub's life. A shopkeeper called Morris Mitchom saw the cartoon and his wife made a soft toy bear, with black buttons for eyes, to put in their shop window. Morris put a sign next to it, saying 'Teddy's Bear'. By 1907, most soft toy bears made in Europe and the USA were called teddy bears.

Steiff bears

Also in 1902, the German toy company, Steiff, made the first toy bear that had jointed arms and legs. It was shown at the Leipzig Toy Fair in 1903. The bear was spotted by an American shopowner who ordered 3,000 Steiff bears to sell back home.

Winnie-the-Pooh

In 1921, Christopher Robin Milne was given a teddy bear for his first birthday. His father, the English author AA Milne, saw how his son loved playing with his bear and decided to write a story about a boy, his teddy bear and other toys. In 1925, *Winnie-the-Pooh* was published. Today, Winnie-the-Pooh remains one of the world's best-known teddy bears.

TIMELINE

1902
Morris Mitchom puts 'Teddy's Bear' in his shop window.

1902
The Steiff toy company makes jointed toy bears to sell at a toy fair. Soon everyone wants a teddy bear.

1920
Teddy bears wearing clothes are made.

1925
Winnie-the-Pooh is published. It is followed by *The House at Pooh Corner*.

1997
The first Build-a-Bear Workshop store is opened in St Louis, USA. At these stores, children can choose, make and dress their own bears.

Board games

Although there are many new and exciting board games available today, some of the most popular games, such as chess and draughts, were invented hundreds, or even thousands, of years ago.

Snakes and Ladders

Snakes and Ladders developed from an ancient Indian game called Moksha-Patamu. The game became popular in England in 1892. It is thought that the game was invented

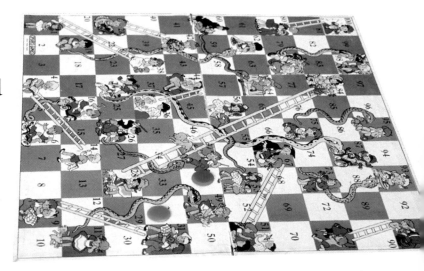

to teach people about good and bad. Moving up a ladder is like doing good because it helps you to go up in life, but going down a snake is like doing something bad because you fall back.

Draughts

The game of draughts probably developed from an Egyptian game called Alquerque, around 600 BCE. It was originally played on stone slabs until someone thought to use a wooden chess board, in around 1100 CE. In the 1600s, the French took to the game, but called it Jeu Force. In the USA it is called checkers.

Chess

No one is certain when chess was invented but it was played in the 8th century in India and in Persia (now Iran). By the 11th century, chess was played in Britain and records show that England's King Canute played it, too. Legend goes that after arguing during a game, he had his opponent killed.

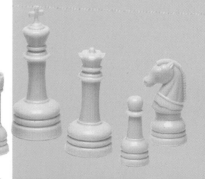

TIMELINE

600 BCE
Draughts is played in Ancient Egypt.

700 CE
Chess is invented in India and quickly spreads to Persia (now Iran).

900s
Chess comes to Europe.

1600s
The French adopt draughts.

1892
Snakes and Ladders becomes popular in England.

1980s
Computer chess games are available.

Jigsaw puzzles

In the shops, you can find jigsaw puzzles for all ages and interests. But have you ever wondered who first had the idea of cutting up a picture that could be joined back together again?

Map puzzles

In 1767, a London mapmaker called John Spilsbury put one of his maps on a large piece of wood and cut around the outside of each country with a saw. He did this so children could learn to piece the countries together to make a map of the world.

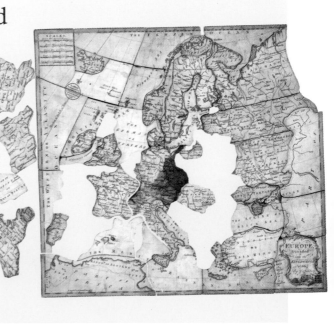

More pictures

At first, jigsaw puzzles were a learning tool. But by 1880, pictures other than maps were being glued onto wood and then cut out with saws. By about 1890, puzzles were made out of cardboard as well as wood. Then, in the 1920s and 1930s, companies like Chad Valley in Britain and Einson-Freeman in the USA began making lots of different kinds of jigsaw puzzles.

Keeping busy

In 1932, during the Great Depression in the USA, a weekly jigsaw puzzle was made and sold like a magazine. At first only 12,000 puzzles were made each week but it soon caught on as a way to pass time cheaply. At one point, puzzle-makers were making up to 200,000 puzzles a week!

TIMELINE

1767
John Spilsbury makes map puzzles.

1880
Pictures other than maps are used for the puzzles.

1890
Jigsaws are made out of cardboard, as well as wood.

1920s–30s
Companies begin mass-producing jigsaw puzzles on a weekly basis.

Late 1950s
Three-dimensional puzzles are made. Instead of building a flat puzzle, the puzzle stands upright.

Yo-yos

It takes a bit of practice to master the yo-yo, but once you get the hang of it, yo-yos are great fun. Some people enter competitions to show off their yo-yo tricks.

Yo-yo fun
In the late 18th century, the French Emperor Napoleon is said to have enjoyed playing with yo-yos to relax.

Ancient yo-yos

Historians think that the yo-yo is one of the oldest toys in the world. In fact, you can see ancient yo-yos, probably made from clay, in pictures found on Ancient Greek artefacts.

Wooden yo-yos

The first wooden yo-yos were made in the Philippines and from the 1400s onwards, they became popular in Africa and Europe. Like many toys, early yo-yos were made by parents for their children.

Donald Duncan's yo-yo company

In 1929, Donald Duncan, from the USA, bought a yo-yo company. He made some improvements to the yo-yo design and then decided to start making yo-yos out of plastic. They were lighter and easier to use. Duncan also sent his staff around the USA to show people how to do yo-yo tricks, creating a yo-yo craze as they went.

100 CE
Yo-yos are used in Ancient Greece.

1400s
Yo-yos are made of wood. They become popular all around the world.

1800s
English children start playing with yo-yos.

1950s
Plastic yo-yos are made by Donald Duncan's company.

1990s
A yo-yo craze sweeps England.

Miniature cars

Miniature cars look just like real cars, only smaller. They have been popular for many years and some people collect them.

Dinky cars

In the early 1900s, the first miniature car, a Model T Ford, was made in the USA by Dowst Brothers Company. Later, in 1931 in Britain, miniature cars were made by Frank Hornby of Meccano Ltd. His company already sold toy train sets (see page 23) so the miniature cars, plus planes and lorries, completed the set. They were called Dinky toys.

'Dink' Dinky
The Dinky toy name is said to have come from the Scottish word, 'dink', meaning 'cute' or 'neat'.

Real cars, only smaller

In the 1950s, a company called Lesney started making Matchbox cars. Matchbox cars were miniature copies of the cars driving along the roads. Many children, and even adults, began collecting them.

Very Hot Wheels

In 1968, a new kind of miniature car came along. It was made by the US toy company Mattel and was called Hot Wheels. These cars were made with low-friction wheels, which meant that they could move faster and further than other toy cars.

TIMELINE

Early 1900s
Dowst Brothers Company makes a miniature Model T.

1931
Frank Hornby designs Dinky toys.

1950s
Matchbox cars appear in shops.

1958
Scalextric, an electric racing car toy that drives on a track, is invented.

1960s
Mattel's Hot Wheels cars start to be popular.

2000s
Miniature cars are still popular and are traded on-line.

Dolls

Dolls come in all shapes and sizes. Some look just like real babies while others are like fashion models. Children have played with dolls for at least 4,000 years. Over time, dolls have been made from rags, wood, wax, china, rubber and plastic, like modern Polly Pocket.

Queen Anne dolls

In the 1600s, many children played with simple wooden dolls. At this time, a special kind of doll was made, known as a 'Queen Anne' doll after the queen of the day. It had splendid dolls' clothes and jointed legs but was made for adults, not children.

China dolls

From the 1840s, many doll-makers started creating china heads, legs and arms for their dolls. In fact, the heads were often sold separately so that the child could choose which head they wanted for their new doll. The china could break so children played carefully with their dolls.

Polly Pocket

In 1983, an Englishman called Chris Wiggs designed a small doll for his daughter. Six years later, the first Polly Pocket appeared in the shops. These tiny plastic dolls with removable clothes are now made by the toy company Mattel.

2000 BCE
Egyptian children play with cloth dolls.

1200 CE
Children have wooden dolls.

1600s
Wooden dolls are made with limbs.

1700s
Dolls are made of wax.

1840s
Dolls are made with soft fabric bodies and china arms, legs and heads.

1900s
Dolls are made of all kinds of materials, including plastic.

1959
Barbie is invented.

1989
The first Polly Pocket doll goes on sale.

Radio-controlled toys

A radio-controlled toy is a model toy, such as an aeroplane, car or boat, that is controlled by a radio transmitter. The transmitter is held by someone at a distance away from the toy so that it appears to move on its own.

Super quick!
Some models run on nitromethane, or nitro for short. This is the same as the fuel used by real dragsters and some racing cars.

Radio-controlled boats

In 1898, a scientist named Nikola Tesla held a public demonstration of the first radio-controlled boat in New York, USA. The steering and propulsion on Tesla's boat could be controlled by radio technology. Today, radio-controlled boats remain popular toys for children and adults alike.

First flight

The first officially recorded model aeroplane flight was made by Britain's Colonel HJ Taplin in 1957. Colonel Taplin created the plane himself.

Spin dizzies

Radio-controlled cars were first made in the 1940s but as the cars could move only in circles, they were called 'spin dizzies'. Then, in 1974, a Japanese company, called Tamiya, started selling models that moved in straight lines, too. This started a new toy craze.

1898
Nikola Tesla gives a demonstration of a radio-controlled boat.

1940s
The first radio-controlled cars appear.

1957
The first radio-controlled aeroplane flight is made by the UK's Colonel Taplin.

1974
Tamiya launches a radio-controlled M4 Sherman Tank, starting a new craze for radio-controlled toys.

1976
Tamiya launches a radio-controlled Porche 934.

2005
Tomy launches a new Herbie the Beetle remote-controlled car to tie in with the film.

Train sets

Soon after steam trains were invented in the 1840s, people invented toy trains for children. They were made from wood and children pushed them across the floor, or pulled them along with string. Today, train sets are made from plastic or metal and use electricity to move about.

Magical Marklin

In 1891, a German toy company called Marklin started selling toy trains and the tracks to go with them. At first the Marklin trains were driven by clockwork, then they were powered by steam. The steam trains were expensive, so only the children of wealthy parents owned them.

Lionel trains

In 1900, the American Joshua Lionel Cowen formed a toy company making trains. The company, called Lionel, still operates today. One of its most recent developments is called RailSounds II which reproduces the actual sounds that trains make.

Frank Hornby's trains

In Britain and France, Frank Hornby's Meccano Ltd led the way in developing electric train sets in the 1920s. They were sold alongside existing clockwork models. Over the next 30 years, electric train sets became popular. Children could buy carriages, figures and other items to go with their train set.

T I M E L I N E

1840s
The first toy trains are made of wood.

1870s
Trains that move by clockwork or steam are sold.

1891
Marklin makes toy trains with tracks.

1900
Lionel Manufacturing Company forms.

1920s
Electric toy trains become popular.

1935
Lionel makes the first train with a whistle sound.

1938
Hornby's Dublo train is sold in clockwork or electric form.

1994
Lionel trains that reproduce train noises are sold.

Skateboards

Skateboards may be quite a recent toy invention, but they are one of the most popular. While many people skateboard for fun, skateboarding is also taken seriously as a sport around the world, with both adults and children taking part.

Skateboarding starts

In 1760, Belgium-born Jean-Joseph Merlin made the first rollerskates. Nearly 150 years later, in the early 1900s, people began fixing rollerskate wheels onto pieces of wood.

Keep covered! Skateboarders' safety has become more important. Today, boarders wear helmets and sometimes knee and elbow pads, too.

Surfing the streets

Skateboarding really took off in the early 1960s when Larry Stevenson of the USA got people to use skateboards to surf the streets. Then, in 1963, his company, 'Mahaka', made the first professional skateboards. Within just a few years, over 50 million skateboards were sold.

All about wheels

The early skateboards had wheels made from clay. These did not grip surfaces very well and many skateboarders had bad accidents. However, in 1973, another American, Frank Nasworthy, introduced plastic wheels which made skateboards much safer.

TIMELINE

1760
Merlin makes the first rollerskates.

Early 1900s
People fit rollerskate wheels onto wood to make skateboards.

1963
The first professional boards are made by the Mahaka company.

1973
Frank Nasworthy designs a plastic wheel which makes skateboards much safer.

1976
The first skateboard park is built in Florida, USA.

1993
The first X Games takes place. These are like the Olympics of extreme sports, including skateboarding.

Computer games

Computer games may be one of the newest toys that we have today, but even they have changed in how they look. They certainly were not as popular when they first appeared.

Warning!
Always check the age rating on computer games and ask an adult for permission before you start playing a computer game.

Spacewar

The first computer game was called Spacewar. It was invented by three American scientists called Russell, Samson and Graetz in 1962. The aim of Spacewar was for spaceships to shoot at each other.

In your hands!

In 1989, hand-held games consoles, such as Game Boy, were invented by Nintendo. One of the most popular games to play was Tetris, where players had to pack different coloured shapes into a grid.

Through the television

Since the 1980s, lots of games and home consoles have been made, many of which use the television screen. These include the Sony Playstation in 2000 and the Microsoft Xbox, launched in 2001. In 2005, the hand-held Sony Playstation was launched (see above). It is small enough to fit in backpacks and briefcases and it can be played with headphones.

TIMELINE

1962
Spacewar is invented.

1974
The tennis game, Pong, becomes available for home use.

1980
Pac-Man is launched by Nintendo.

1989
Game Boy consoles and Tetris go on sale.

1994
CD-ROM games for home computers become popular.

2000
Playstation One is made by the Sony Corporation.

2001
Microsoft Xbox is launched.

2005
A portable Playstation is launched by Sony.

Other inventions

There are many other toys and games that people play with. Some were invented such a long time ago that we do not know the inventor. Building blocks, kites and skipping ropes fall into this group.

Building blocks

Children have played with building blocks for hundreds of years. At first, children used stones as building blocks but later, in the Victorian era, blocks were made from wood. Today, there is a huge variety of building toys, from plastic Lego and K'nex to magnetic Geomags.

Kites

It is thought that kites were invented by the Chinese 3,000 years ago. They were made out of silk and bamboo. Today, there are many different kinds of kite, such as stunt kites and huge kites for kite-surfing. Some of today's kites have nylon sails fixed to fibre-glass frames.

Skipping ropes

Skipping has been popular since the 1800s. Then, skipping ropes had wooden handles and many children played complicated skipping games with friends. Although some of today's ropes also have wooden handles, most are now plastic.

PLASTIC

Plastic is one of the most common materials for making toys – without it, many of the toys in this book would not be possible.

Plastic is used to make toys because it is tough, safe, waterproof, easily moulded and it can be brightly coloured.

Plastic was accidentally discovered by two chemists, J Paul Hogan and Robert L Banks. While the chemists were trying to make fuel, they realised that their equipment had become clogged up with a sticky, white substance. They recreated the white substance and realised that it was a new material.

Timeline

2000 BCE
Egyptian children play with cloth dolls, marbles, spinning tops and pull-along toys.

700 CE
Chess is played in India and Persia (Iran).

1200 CE
Children have wooden dolls.

1400s
Yo-yos are made of wood.

1600s
Jointed dolls are invented.

1700s
Dolls are made of wax.

1767
John Spilsbury makes the first jigsaw puzzle.

1840s
The first toy trains are made from wood.

1870s
Trains are made out of tin and are moved by clockwork or steam.

1890
Jigsaws are made out of cardboard, as well as wood.

1892
Snakes and Ladders becomes popular in England.

1898
Nikola Tesla demonstrates a radio-controlled boat.

Early 1900s
The first skateboards are made.

1902

Morris Mitchom displays a 'Teddy's bear' in his shop.

1929

Donald Duncan buys a yo-yo company.

1931

Dinky cars appear.

1950s

Matchbox makes miniature cars.

1957

A radio-controlled plane flies.

1959

The Barbie doll is invented.

1960s

Hot Wheels friction cars start to be popular.

1962

The first computer game, Spacewar, is invented in the USA.

1974

The video game, Pong, is launched for home use.

1989

The first Polly Pocket doll goes on sale.

1989

Game Boy consoles go on sale. The game Tetris becomes very popular.

2000

Playstation One is made by the Sony Corporation.

2001

Microsoft Xbox is launched.

Glossary

Clay
A material found in the Earth that hardens when it is heated. Clay can be moulded and hardened to make many things.

Clockwork
The way a toy train is powered or made to move. This could be by weights pulling down or coiled-up springs slowly unwinding.

Consoles
The main part of a computer game in which the operating system is found.

Craze
When a toy is in fashion, it is the latest craze.

Fibreglass
A material made up of very fine fibres of glass.

Great Depression
The time from 1929 through the 1930s when the USA lost a lot of money and people were poor.

Historians
People who study and write about history.

Low-friction wheels
Wheels with little resistance between them and the surface they are moving on. This means that the wheels can turn faster.

Patented
When someone owns the rights to an invention so that it cannot be copied by other inventors.

Plastic
A material used to make many toys. Plastic is waterproof and long-lasting.

Propulsion
When something is propelled or moved forwards.

Radio transmitter
A device that transfers radio waves from one machine or gadget to another.

Three-dimensional
Having three dimensions: length, width and height.

Victorian era
The time when Queen Victoria of England was on the throne, between 1837 and 1901.

Websites

www.nationalgeographic.com/features/96/inventions
Have loads of fun with games about inventions.

http://home.howstuffworks.com
Find out how everyday inventions work by searching for them on this website.

www.uspto.gov/web/offices/ac/ahrpa/opa/kids/index.html
Visit the American Patent and Trademark Office's website to find out more about inventions and how they are patented.

www.hants.gov.uk/museum/toys/history/toy_cars.html
Explore the Hampshire Museum's great collection of toys.

www.vam.ac.uk/moc
Visit the Museum of Childhood, for a virtual tour of its collections.

www.historychannel.com/exhibits/toys/index.html
Read all about your favourite toys, who invented them and how they work.

www.yo-yo.com
Find out all about Duncan yo-yos - from the first models to the latest yo-yo crazes. Click on 'multimedia' for loads of fun yo-yo games, downloads and art.

www.mattel.com/our_toys
Look at the websites of all your favourite Mattel toys, including Hot Wheels, Matchbox cars, Barbie and Polly Pocket.

Note to parents:
Every effort has been made by the publishers to ensure that the websites in this book are suitable for children, that they are of the highest educational value, and that they contain no inappropriate or offensive material. However, due to the nature of the Internet, it is impossible to guarantee that the contents of these sites will not be altered. We strongly advise that Internet access is supervised by a responsible adult.

Index

SHORT TALES
Fairy Tales

Jack and the Beanstalk

Adapted by J.J. Hart
Illustrated by Mike Dubisch

WAYLAND

WAYLAND

First published in 2013 by Wayland

Copyright © 2013 Wayland

Wayland
338 Euston Road
London NW1 3BH

Wayland Australia
Level 17/207 Kent Street
Sydney, NSW 2000

Adapted Text by J. J. Hart
Illustrations by Mike Dubisch
Colours by Wes Hartman
Edited by Stephanie Hedlund
Interior Layout by Kristen Fitzner Denton and Alyssa Peacock
Book Design and Packaging by Shannon Eric Denton
Cover Design by Alyssa Peacock

Copyright © 2008 by Abdo Consulting Group

A cataloguing record for this title is available at the British Library.
Dewey number: 823.9'2

Printed in China

ISBN: 978 0 7502 7751 8

Wayland is a division of Hachette Children's Books, an Hachette UK company.
www.hachette.co.uk

Jack and his mother had no money and no food.

All they had to sell was their cow, which gave them milk.

'Take her to market' said Jack's mother. 'We need money to buy food to eat.'

So Jack led the cow to the market.

On the way, he met a man.

The man offered to buy Jack's cow.

'I will trade you these five magic beans for her,' said the man. 'They will grow right up to the sky.'

Jack could hardly believe his luck.

But Jack's mother didn't believe in magic beans.

She was very angry. 'You sold our cow for five beans?' she cried.

'Not just any beans, Mother' said Jack. 'Magic beans.'

Jack's mother threw the beans out of the window.

'There are no such things as magic beans, Jack'
said Jack's mother. 'Now we don't have any milk
or any money.'

Jack went to bed without
any supper.

In the morning, he found that
the man had been right! The
beans were magic, after all!

The beanstalks had grown right
up through the clouds, higher
than Jack could see.

Jack wanted to see how high they went.

He climbed and he climbed and he climbed.

Soon, he could not see his own house.

Above the clouds was a wonderful land.

Jack had never seen anything like it.

He decided to visit the richest, grandest house in sight.

A great big giant woman was sweeping outside the house.

'Good morning' said Jack.

Jack had not had dinner or breakfast, and he was very hungry.

'Have you anything to eat?' Jack asked the woman.

The woman was nice. She invited Jack inside.

Jack was amazed at how big everything in the house was!

The giant's wife gave him bread, milk and a piece of cheese. He sat on the floor to eat.

But soon the whole house began to shake.

It was the giant!

The giant's wife hid Jack inside her oven, just in time.

'Cook these for me, wife!' roared the giant. The giant started to leave the kitchen, but then he stopped and sniffed.

'Fee-fi-fo-fum,

I smell the blood of an Englishman,

Be he alive or be he dead,

I'll grind his bones to make my bread.'

'Nonsense, dear' said the giant's wife. 'Go and wash your hands and I'll make your breakfast.'

She took Jack from the oven and hid him in a cupboard.

There, Jack waited. The giant ate and then sat at the table counting his gold. Soon, he fell asleep.

Jack knew his mother could buy food with the gold. The giant would never miss one bag.

Jack took a bag of gold and ran.

He raced back down the beanstalk.

At the bottom, he showed his mother the gold.

'See, Mother?' said Jack. 'I told you the beans were magic.'

Jack and his mother lived off the gold for months.
But one day it ran out.

Jack went back up the beanstalk to see what else
he could find.

The giant's wife was outside her house again.

'Please,' said Jack, who was hungry from his long climb. 'May I have some bread?'

The woman was nice and she fed Jack again.

21

Soon, the giant returned.

'Fee-fi-fo-fum,
I smell the blood of an Englishman,
Be he alive or be he dead,
I'll grind his bones to make my bread.'

'Nonsense, dear' said the giant's wife. 'Go and wash, and I'll make your lunch.'

When the giant left, the woman hid Jack in the cupboard.

After his lunch, the giant put a hen on the table.
'Lay' he said. The hen laid an egg of gold.

Jack knew those golden eggs would buy plenty
of food!

He waited until the giant had fallen fast asleep.

Then Jack took the hen. He climbed down the beanstalk as fast as he could.

When he arrived home he said 'Those magic beans have given us another treasure. This hen lays golden eggs!'

The hen laid a golden egg every day. Jack and his mother were able to buy all the food they needed.

But Jack wanted to see what other wonders waited at the top of the beanstalk.

A week later, he climbed up again.

He found the giant's wife and she invited him inside. Again he hid in the cupboard.

After the giant ate, a magical golden harp sang a song for him. The giant fell fast asleep.

Jack crept out of hiding to see the harp.

'Master, master!' called the magical harp, as soon as Jack held it.

The giant woke up. Jack was frightened! He ran, still holding the harp.

The giant saw him and gave chase.

Jack hurried down the beanstalk as fast as he could.

'Mother, bring me an axe!' Jack called when he neared the bottom.

She met him with an axe.

Jack gave the beanstalk a mighty chop. It fell over and the giant fell with it.

Safe at home, Jack knew he would never visit the giant's house in the clouds again.

SHORT TALES
Fables

Titles in the Short Tales Fables series:

The Ants and the Grasshopper

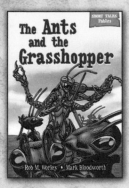

978 0 7502 7756 3

The Boy Who Cried Wolf

978 0 7502 7757 0

The Fox and the Grapes

978 0 7502 7758 7

The Lion and the Mouse

978 0 7502 7783 9

The Tortoise and the Hare

978 0 7502 7784 6

The Town Mouse and the Country Mouse

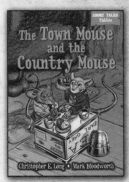

978 0 7502 7785 3

WAYLAND
www.waylandbooks.co.uk

Follow us on Twitter @waylandbooks | Find us on Facebook Wayland Books

SHORT TALES
Fairy Tales

Titles in the Short Tales Fairy Tales series:

Aladdin and the Lamp

978 0 7502 7750 1

Beauty and the Beast

978 0 7502 7752 5

Jack and the Beanstalk

978 0 7502 7751 8

Puss in Boots

978 0 7502 7754 9

Sleeping Beauty

978 0 7502 7755 6

The Little Mermaid

978 0 7502 7753 2

WAYLAND
www.waylandbooks.co.uk

Follow us on Twitter @waylandbooks | Find us on Facebook Wayland Books

ASTRONAUT TRAVEL GUIDES

MERCURY and VENUS

ISABEL THOMAS

www.raintreepublishers.co.uk
Visit our website to find out
more information about
Raintree books.

To order:
☎ Phone 0845 6044371
🖷 Fax +44 (0) 1865 312263
✉ Email myorders@raintreepublishers.co.uk

Customers from outside the UK please telephone +44 1865 312262

Raintree is an imprint of Capstone Global Library
Limited, a company incorporated in England and
Wales having its registered office at 7 Pilgrim
Street, London, EC4V 6LB – Registered company
number: 6695582

Text © Capstone Global Library Limited 2013
First published in hardback in 2013
The moral rights of the proprietor have been
asserted.

Edited by Nancy Dickmann and Laura Knowles
Designed by Steve Mead
Original illustrations © Capstone Global
   Library Ltd 2013
Picture research by Mica Brancic
Originated by Capstone Global Library Ltd
Printed and bound in China by CTPS

ISBN 978 1 406 23975 1 (hardback)
16 15 14 13 12
10 9 8 7 6 5 4 3 2 1

British Library Cataloguing in Publication Data
Thomas, Isabel
Mercury and Venus. – (Astronaut travel guides)
523.4'1-dc23
A full catalogue record for this book is available
from the British Library.

Acknowledgements
We would like to thank the following for
permission to reproduce photographs: Alamy
p. 6 (© The Print Collector); Brown University
p. 17 (Vernadsky Institute/O. de Goursac);
Corbis pp. 8 (The Art Archive/© Alfredo Dagli
Orti), 23 (Sygma/© Tony Korody), 38 (© kyodo/
Xinhua Press); ESA pp. 5 bottom and 34, 39
(Astrium); Getty Images p. 29 (De Agostini/DEA
/D'ARCO EDITORI); © Jia Hao p. 7; NASA pp.
4 (© Calvin J Hamilton), 5 top and 16 (Johns
Hopkins University Applied Physics Laboratory),
10 (Ames Research Center), 12, 14 (JPL), 18,
25 (JPL-Caltech/University of Arizona), 28 (Johns
Hopkins University Applied Physics Laboratory/
Arizona State University/Carnegie Institution
of Washington. Image reproduced courtesy of
Science/AAAS.), 30 (JPL), 31, 32, 33 (JPL), 37
(JPL/USGS); Science Photo Library pp. 9 (David
Parker), 19 (Christian Darkin), 21 (Detlev Van
Ravenswaay), 26 (Walter Myers); Shutterstock
pp. 40-41 (© Martiin || Fluidworkshop); The
Bridgeman Art Library p. 11 (National Geographic
Society/Jean-Leon Huens).

Design image elements reproduced with
permission of Shutterstock/© Benjamin Haas/
© Luis Stortini Sabor aka Cvadrat/© Mopic/
© Stephen Coburn.

Cover photograph of a 3D perspective View
of the Eistla Region of Venus reproduced with
permission of NASA.

We would like to thank Mark Thompson, Paolo
Nespoli, and ESA for their invaluable help in the
preparation of this book.

Every effort has been made to contact copyright
holders of material reproduced in this book.
Any omissions will be rectified in subsequent
printings if notice is given to the publisher.

CONTENTS

Some words are shown in bold, **like this**. You can find out what they mean by looking in the glossary.

DON'T FORGET

These boxes will remind you what you need to take with you on your big adventure.

NUMBER CRUNCHING

Don't miss these little chunks of data as you whizz through the travel guide!

AMAZING FACTS

You need to know these fascinating facts to get the most out of your space safari!

WHO'S WHO?

Find out about the space explorers who have studied the universe in the past and today.

VISITING MERCURY AND VENUS

Adventurous astronauts will love visiting Mercury and Venus. From chilly **craters** to violent volcanoes, these planets are packed with spectacular sights.

Be prepared for hideous heat and clouds made of acid on Venus.

WHERE ARE THEY?

Mercury and Venus are the only planets in our **solar system** that are closer to the Sun than Earth is. This makes them seriously hot! Mercury is the closest planet to the Sun, and is only slightly larger than our Moon. Venus is Earth's closest neighbour, and is around the same size as our planet. Most of the unmanned spacecraft that visit Mercury and Venus take in both planets in a single trip.

WHY GO?

Along with Earth and Mars, Mercury and Venus are known as the rocky planets. Like Earth, they both have a solid, rocky surface that an astronaut can walk on. But when you step out of your spaceship, you'll discover two very different worlds.

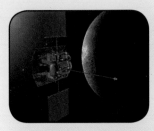

See pages 14–17 to find out which spacecraft have visited Mercury and Venus.

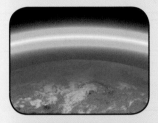

Discover what the atmosphere is like on Venus on pages 26–27.

Meet astronaut Paolo Nespoli on page 34.

NUMBER CRUNCHING

Compared to most planets, Venus is a short hop away. In 2005, the space **probe** *Venus Express* made the journey to Venus in 155 days. It will take you longer to get to Mercury. The *Mercury Messenger* probe, launched in August 2004, reached the planet in January 2008.

EXPLORING MERCURY AND VENUS FROM EARTH

It's not just astronauts who are interested in Mercury and Venus. Humans have been gazing at the planets and trying to uncover their secrets for thousands of years.

EARLY ASTROLOGY

Mercury and Venus can be spotted from Earth in the evening and early morning. They look like very large, bright stars. Ancient peoples didn't know what planets and stars were, but they began to notice patterns in their movements across the sky. They recorded the patterns and used the **data** to create calendars and to try to predict the future. This is known as astrology.

More than 2,500 years ago, the Mayans believed that Venus was as important as the Sun. They called the planet *Xux Ek*, meaning the "Great Star" and kept careful records of when it appeared in the sky.

NAMING THE PLANETS

Many ancient cultures linked the objects they saw in the sky to religion. Early **astronomers** were often priests, and the planets were named after gods and goddesses.

The names that we use today come from Roman **mythology**. Mercury was the Roman messenger god who wore winged sandals so he could speed through the sky. Mercury suits this name because it also moves quickly across the sky. Sunlight bounces off thick clouds around Venus, making it look like a beautiful shining star. It is named after the Roman goddess of love and beauty.

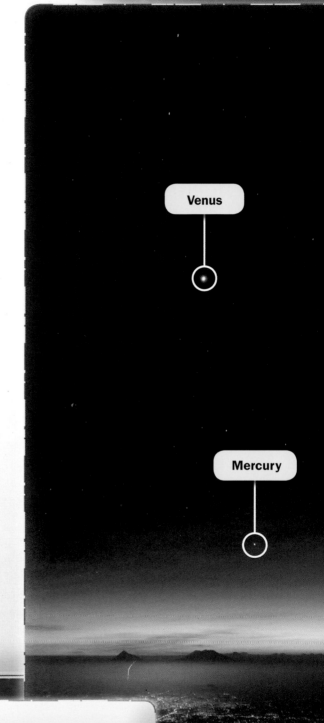

Venus

Mercury

Venus was known as the Morning Star and Evening Star because it looks so bright in the sky at dawn and dusk. Mercury is much harder to spot.

THE SCIENCE OF ASTRONOMY

Although the movement of planets cannot be used to predict human events, the information collected by early astrologers was very useful. Astronomers used it to discover new things about the planets and Earth itself.

GREEK STAR-GAZING

From around 450 BC, the ancient Greeks changed how the planets and stars were studied. Many Greek astronomers were mathematicians. They came up with new ideas about what Mercury and Venus were, and why they appeared to move through the sky. Some of their ideas were right, but others we now know are wrong.

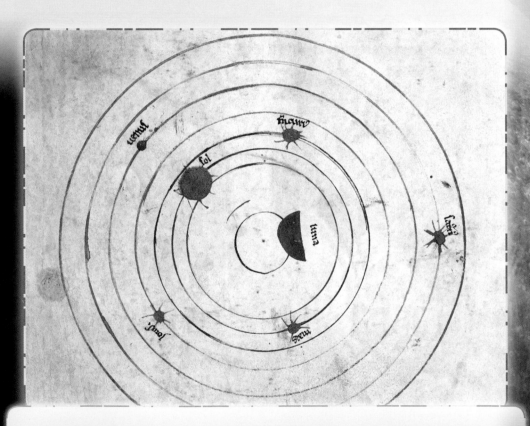

Greek astronomer Ptolemy wrongly thought that the planets, Sun, Moon, and stars travelled around Earth. This idea lasted for 1,400 years!

ARABIC SCHOLARS

From the AD 600s, Arabic astronomers made many important discoveries. They studied ancient Greek ideas about the solar system. They built huge **observatories**. The most famous Arab astronomer is al-Battani. He made superb **instruments** to track the movement of planets, and work out their positions.

COPERNICUS AND KEPLER

Al-Battani's work was very helpful to European scientists. In the 1500s, Nicolaus Copernicus made a huge breakthrough. He suggested that the planets, including Earth, actually travelled around the Sun.

Later, the scientist Johannes Kepler combined Copernicus' ideas with accurate data to explain how the planets move through space. This can be used to predict where Mercury and Venus will be at any time – important information for a modern-day astronaut trying to get there!

Astrolabes were the laptop computers of the past! They were used to measure the position of objects in the sky, and tell the time of the day or year.

WHO'S WHO?

The Greek mathematician Pythagoras (c. 580–c.500 BC) noticed that the Morning Star and Evening Star were actually the same object: Venus. He was also probably the first to suggest that all planets are spheres (ball-shaped).

A BETTER VIEW OF THE PLANETS

Until the 1600s, astronomers could only see the planets as well as you can with your eyes. When the **telescope** was invented in 1609, it was suddenly possible to make planets and stars look much nearer. This allowed scientists to see surprising new details.

In 1610, Galileo Galilei used telescopes to make an amazing discovery. He saw that Venus had phases (appeared to change shape) like the Moon. Galileo knew that this could only happen if planets **orbit** the Sun, not Earth. He had proved that Copernicus was right.

Through his telescopes, Galileo could see different amounts of Venus' sunlit side at different times. The race was now on to invent better telescopes and make new findings.

NEW DISCOVERIES

During the 1800s, astronomers developed instruments and techniques that helped them to discover more about planets. From the 1850s, people used cameras to record the images seen through telescopes, instead of drawing them by hand. Enough detail could be seen to create rough maps of Mercury's surface. But even though Venus is closer to Earth than Mercury, the surface of Venus remained a mystery, hidden behind its thick clouds.

Astronomers began to explore the **Universe** beyond our solar system. However, an exciting development would soon bring attention back to Mercury, Venus, and the other planets: space travel.

WHO'S WHO?

Italian scientist Galileo Galilei (1564–1642) was the first person to use telescopes to study the sky. His proof that planets orbit the Sun went against the beliefs of the Roman Catholic Church, which was very powerful at that time. In 1633, Galileo was put on trial, and ordered to stay inside his house for the rest of his life.

INTERVIEW WITH AN ASTRONOMER

Mark Thompson has been an amateur astronomer for 20 years. As a presenter on BBC's *The One Show* and *Stargazing LIVE*, he helps adults and young people to understand the night sky.

Q *What made you want to be an astronomer in the first place?*

A I think it was actually a view of Saturn through a telescope. My dad took me to my local observatory when I was probably about ten years old. As luck would have it, I got to see Saturn through a telescope, and to see it for real – it wasn't in a book, it wasn't on a TV screen, it wasn't from a space craft – you know, to see it for real with its rings was a sight that absolutely fired my imagination and it's stayed with me ever since. It seemed like it was the best view I've ever had of Saturn because it was the first. It was absolutely the sight of Saturn that just sparked that imagination, and set me on the journey that I had.

Q What is your favourite planet, and why?

A I would probably say Mars. The reason I say Mars is because it changes. When you look through a telescope, you can actually see things changing. Mars has polar caps, and as Mars goes through its seasons like we have on the Earth, you can actually see the polar caps growing and shrinking. You can see dust storms and, because Mars is like one big desert, sometimes these big dust storms whip up and obscure (hide) all the detail from the surface.

Q Have you got any space heroes?

A I think Galileo would have to be one. He was the first one to use a telescope on the night sky. I think he was probably one of the key people who made some big, big, big discoveries that changed our view of the Universe. And, you know, he paid for it. He got arrested by the church and stuck in house arrest for a lot of years. But I think the things he did, and people like him, took us forwards in leaps and bounds in understanding the Universe.

Q What advice would you give to readers who want to be astronomers?

A I would say, obviously, go with a responsible adult, don't go out on your own at night time. Use a pair of binoculars or a small telescope if you can get one. Just start looking, because there's an incredible world out there. If you can, either buy a planisphere or get one of these smart phone applications and start learning your way around the sky, and get out there and enjoy it. You know, there's loads of stuff that's in the sky that you can see that's really easy to find. It's a fantastic pastime and it means you can stay up late as well!

THE SPACE AGE

The first space flights took place in the mid-1900s, starting with trips into Earth's orbit. Countries began competing to explore the solar system.

Telescopes were sent into orbit around Earth, where they had a much better view of space. Robotic probes were sent to the planets. They used cameras, **radar**, and other instruments to collect as much information as possible.

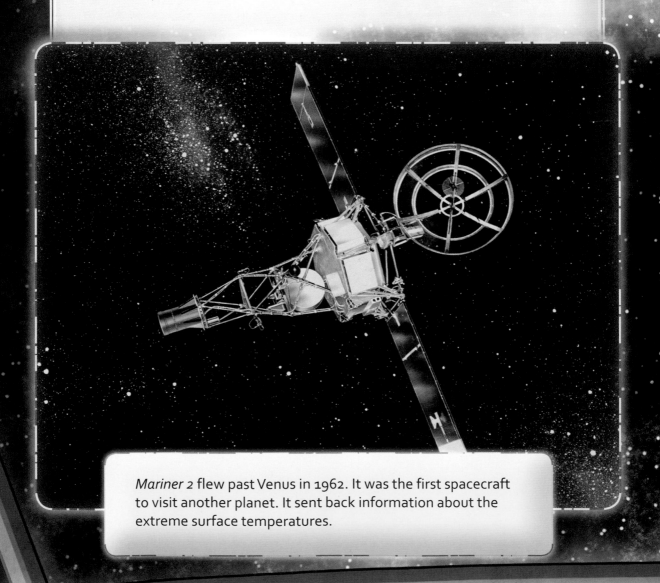

Mariner 2 flew past Venus in 1962. It was the first spacecraft to visit another planet. It sent back information about the extreme surface temperatures.

GETTING THERE

When you fly to Mercury and Venus, you will have to overcome the challenges faced by the first robotic probes.

- Escaping Earth: A force called **gravity** attracts objects to each other. Bigger objects have stronger gravity. It is Earth's gravity that stops everything on it from floating off into space. Rockets are used to overcome this force and blast probes into space.

- Finding the planets: Venus zooms through space at 35 kilometres (22 miles) per second, and Mercury is even faster at 50 kilometres (31 miles) per second. That is a solar system record! They don't stay in one place for long.

- Coping with heat: Mercury and Venus are much closer to the Sun so you will need a super-tough spaceship and spacesuit to protect you from roasting heat and dangerous **radiation**.

AMAZING FACTS

Other planets are very hard to get to, even with robotic spacecraft. Humans were able to explore the Moon on foot before probes managed to photograph the surfaces of Mercury and Venus!

PHOTOGRAPHING THE PLANETS

Information collected by Venus and Mercury missions will help you on your own journey. You may even come across the remains of these probes.

MAPPING MERCURY

In 1974 and 1975, **NASA**'s *Mariner 10* probe took the first close-up photographs of Mercury's surface. In 2004, NASA launched the *Mercury Messenger* mission. Its tasks include looking for frozen water in deep craters on Mercury. It has sent back thousands of pictures of the surface.

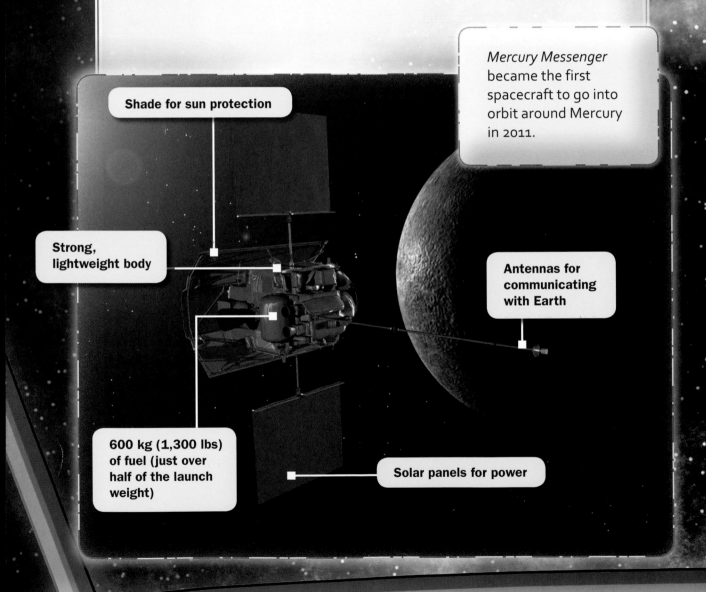

Mercury Messenger became the first spacecraft to go into orbit around Mercury in 2011.

Shade for sun protection

Strong, lightweight body

Antennas for communicating with Earth

600 kg (1,300 lbs) of fuel (just over half of the launch weight)

Solar panels for power

Flat slabs of rock

Soil

Venera 13 managed to take this photo of Venus' surface, before being destroyed by heat and **pressure**.

VISITING VENUS

Mariner 2 flew by Venus in 1962, and *Mariner 10* managed to snap a close-up on its way to Mercury. However, thick clouds made the surface invisible. No one knew what it looked like until 1975, when two *Venera* probes, sent by the **Soviet Union**, managed to land. They sent back a few black and white photographs. In 1981, two more *Venera* probes took colour photographs and even studied the soil.

NASA's *Pioneer Venus* and *Magellan* probes used radar to "see through" Venus's clouds. Between 1990 and 1994, Magellan mapped 98 per cent of the surface. The latest probe to visit Venus was the European **Space Agency**'s (ESA) *Venus Express*, which began orbiting the planet in 2006. Its mission was to study Venus' **atmosphere**. It also made the exciting discovery that volcanoes on Venus may still be active.

ALL ABOUT MERCURY AND VENUS

Scientists combined the amazing discoveries of Mercury and Venus probes with observations made from Earth. They worked out what each planet is made of, and what conditions are like on the surface. These are the facts you need to know before you go.

Mercury and Venus took tens of millions of years to form. Around 4.5 billion years ago, collections of rocky **particles** were smashed together in enormous collisions, forming huge lumps of **molten** rock and metal. Large parts of the planets have become solid as they cool.

Mercury's rocky, cratered surface looks a bit like the Moon's.

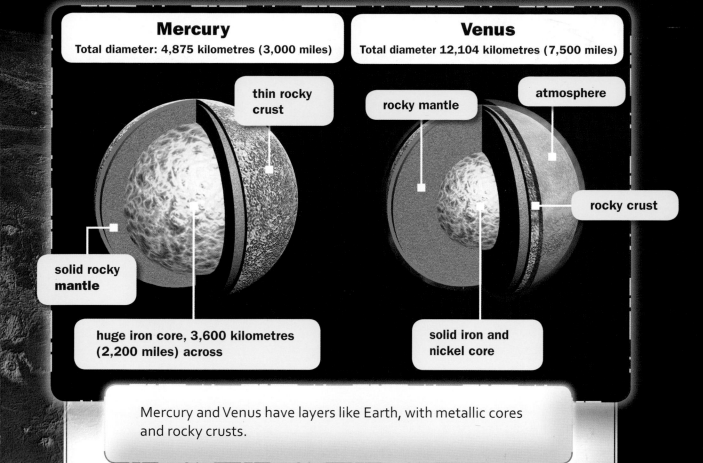

Mercury
Total diameter: 4,875 kilometres (3,000 miles)

Venus
Total diameter 12,104 kilometres (7,500 miles)

thin rocky crust

rocky mantle

atmosphere

rocky crust

solid rocky mantle

huge iron core, 3,600 kilometres (2,200 miles) across

solid iron and nickel core

Mercury and Venus have layers like Earth, with metallic cores and rocky crusts.

METALLIC MERCURY

Mercury is packed with metals, especially iron. Its huge iron **core** is much bigger than expected for such a small planet. Scientists think that Mercury was once much bigger. One idea is that a giant **asteroid** blew off a large portion of the rocky **crust**. Another idea is that a sudden increase in the Sun's heat boiled off some of Mercury's surface!

VOLCANIC VENUS

Venus is a similar size to Earth, and is thought to be similar on the inside. Like Earth, it is still very hot at the centre. The heat melts rocks deep inside Venus. In the past, the molten rock has exploded onto the surface as volcanoes.

RESET YOUR BODY CLOCK

Like Earth, Mercury and Venus are orbiting (travelling around) the Sun, and spinning on their own **axes** at the same time. This means they have years, days, and nights. But the timings are very different from what you are used to.

Each trip that a planet takes around the Sun is known as a year. Because Mercury and Venus are closer to the Sun than Earth, it takes them less time to travel around it. Mercury has the shortest year – astronauts on Mercury would celebrate New Year every 3 months!

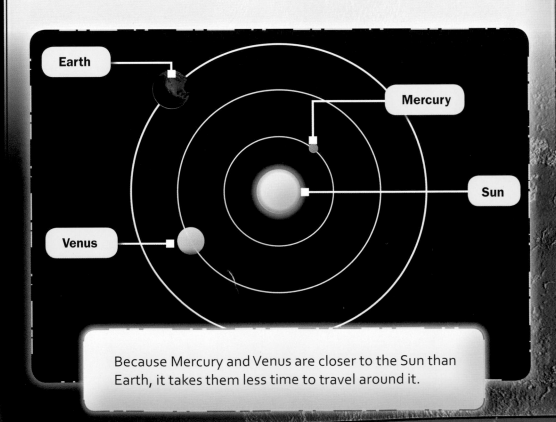

Earth

Mercury

Sun

Venus

Because Mercury and Venus are closer to the Sun than Earth, it takes them less time to travel around it.

Mercury's egg-shaped orbit and slow rotation mean that in some places, the morning Sun rises briefly, sets, and rises again! The same thing happens at sunset.

IN A SPIN

Both planets spin as they travel, causing day and night. Mercury and Venus turn much more slowly than Earth.

Mercury can make two trips around the Sun in the time it takes to spin three times on its axis. Venus is the slowest-spinning planet in our solar system. It takes 243 Earth days to complete one spin. On Venus, a day (one spin) is longer than a year (one trip around the Sun)!

NUMBER CRUNCHING

Planet	Length of orbit/year	Time taken to spin once on axis (day)
Mercury	88 Earth days	59 Earth days
Venus	225 Earth days	243 Earth days
Earth	365 days	24 hours

WHO'S GOING WITH YOU?

If you could put together a dream crew for your mission to Mercury and Venus, it might include some of these people.

CREW MEMBER:

ALBERT EINSTEIN (1879–1955)

Mercury has a "wobbly" orbit that changes position every time the planet circles the Sun. German scientist Einstein worked out why, and correctly predicted how much Mercury's orbit would move. He could help you find Mercury.

POTENTIAL JOB:

Navigator

CREW MEMBER:

EUGENIOS ANTONIADI (1870–1944)

French astronomer Antoniadi became famous for his observations of planets using a telescope on Earth. In 1933, he was the first person to produce a detailed map of the surface of Mercury. His map gave us a lot of information about Mercury, although he did get some things wrong. Antoniadi named some of the surface features you will visit, and a ridge is named after him.

POTENTIAL JOB:

Tour guide on Mercury

CREW MEMBER:

CARL SAGAN (1934–1996)

American astronomer Sagan worked on preparing early missions to Mercury and Venus. He made many important discoveries and helped to work out why Venus is so hot. Most famously, he researched alien life and would know what signs to look out for!

POTENTIAL JOB:

Alien spotter/weather forecaster

CREW MEMBER:

NEIL ARMSTRONG (BORN 1930)

Mercury's cratered surface, low gravity, and thin atmosphere are similar to those on the Moon. Neil Armstrong was the first human to walk on the Moon. He could be a great help.

POTENTIAL JOB:

Health and safety officer

CREW MEMBER:

VOLCANOLOGIST

A volcanologist would be able to help you deal with the harsh conditions on volcanic Venus, such as intense heat and clouds of stinky **sulphur dioxide**. A volcanologist would also be able to spot signs of active volcanoes!

POTENTIAL JOB:

Hazard spotting on Venus

TOUCHING DOWN

A planet's atmosphere is shaped by its size and distance from the Sun. What can you expect as you touch down on Mercury and Venus?

MERCURY'S THIN AIR

On Earth we don't worry that the air we breathe is about to escape into space. But on Mercury, this is happening all the time! Mercury's small size means that it doesn't have enough gravity to trap gases for long. As the planet heats up in the sunlight, these gases zoom off into space.

HARSH CONDITIONS

The lack of atmosphere makes Mercury's surface a harsh place to be. There is nothing to protect the planet from objects hurtling towards it in space. Craters from crashing **meteoroids** cover Mercury's dark and dusty surface. With nothing to shield the planet from the Sun, daytime temperatures rise to 430 degrees Celsius (800 degrees Fahrenheit). That is hotter than an oven. At night, there is nothing to stop this heat escaping into space, so temperatures plunge to –180 degrees Celsius (–290 degrees Fahrenheit) – cold enough to freeze air!

DON'T FORGET

Bring a hard hat in case of meteoroid showers. Mercury's thin atmosphere doesn't "burn up" these pieces of falling dust and rock like Earth's atmosphere does. Objects as small as a grain of sand or as large as a boulder will hit the surface – or your head!

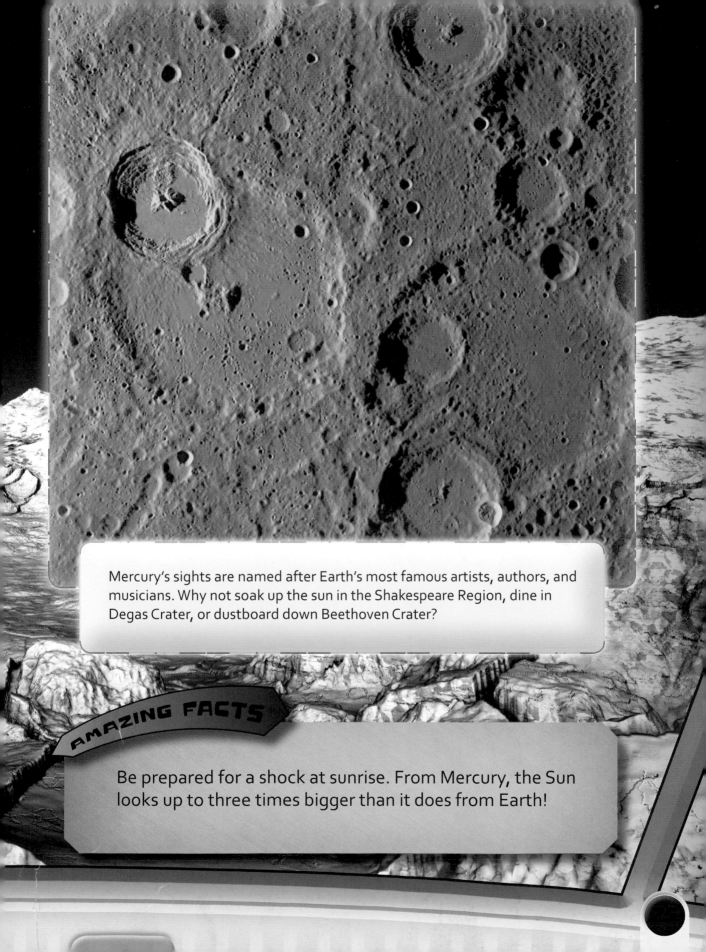

Mercury's sights are named after Earth's most famous artists, authors, and musicians. Why not soak up the sun in the Shakespeare Region, dine in Degas Crater, or dustboard down Beethoven Crater?

AMAZING FACTS

Be prepared for a shock at sunrise. From Mercury, the Sun looks up to three times bigger than it does from Earth!

VENUS

Landing on Venus means passing through fierce winds, clouds of sulphuric acid, and lightning. The surface is no more welcoming. Jagged rocks, enormous volcanoes, and scorched sand dunes are lit by a gloomy, orange glow.

AWFUL ATMOSPHERE

Venus has the opposite problem to Mercury. Its atmosphere is so thick and heavy that it presses down on the surface like a huge weight. The pressure at the surface is 90 times greater than it is on Earth. An astronaut would feel the same pressure as a diver deep under the ocean.

This artist's impression of Venus does not capture the nasty smell. Just like volcanoes on Earth, Venus' atmosphere smells like rotten eggs!

Venus is wrapped in a blanket of clouds 25 kilometres (15 miles) thick. The lower layers are made up of large drops of sulphuric acid, which can burn skin and **dissolve** metal. Acid rain falls from the clouds, but turns into a gas again before it hits the surface of Venus.

An extreme greenhouse effect keeps Venus hotter than Mercury, even though it is nearly twice as far from the Sun.

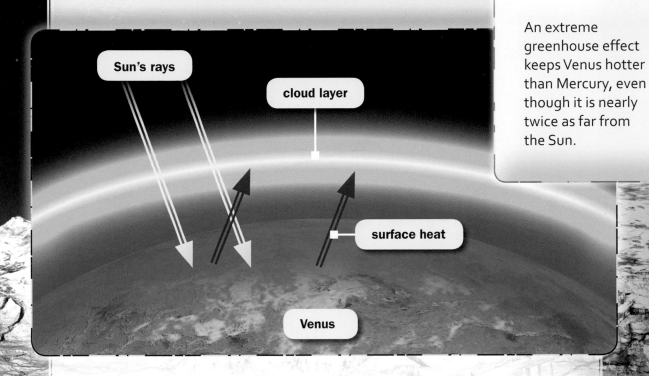

Sun's rays

cloud layer

surface heat

Venus

EXTREME HEAT

Thick clouds mean that Venus is always overcast. Just a fifth of the sunlight reaching Venus gets through to the surface. The clouds reflect most of the sunlight back into space. However, this doesn't help to keep the surface cool. The thick clouds trap the Sun's heat like glass traps heat in a greenhouse. This greenhouse effect keeps surface temperatures at around 464 degrees Celsius (867 degrees Fahrenheit), even at night. It makes Venus the hottest planet in the solar system.

TOP SIGHTS TO SEE

Mercury's surface has been battered and cracked by natural processes. They created the famous features that you'll see on your tour.

RIDGES AND CLIFFS

Mercury is criss-crossed with cliffs up to 3 kilometres (2 miles) high and hundreds of kilometres long. These steep ridges formed as the planet cooled and shrank, causing the crust to crack.

GHOST CRATERS

Mercury's surface is covered with craters, formed by asteroid and meteoroid strikes more than 3.5 billion years ago. Between the craters lie huge, flat plains of lava that oozed out of volcanic vents and cooled in pools. In some places, the solidified lava is several kilometres thick. Some "ghost craters" have been filled in by flowing lava.

The Caloris Basin (shown here as a big, yellow area) is one of the largest craters in the solar system.

CALORIS BASIN

Around 3.8 billion years ago, an asteroid landed on Mercury, forming the huge Caloris Basin. The asteroid that created Caloris was at least 100 kilometres (62 miles) wide, and it left a crater 1,550 kilometres (960 miles) across.

Caloris is one of the hottest places on Mercury – the name means "heat" in Latin. The basin floor is covered with small volcanoes, craters, and trenches. Visit the Brahms Crater to see the 3-kilometre (2-mile) high mountain peak in the centre.

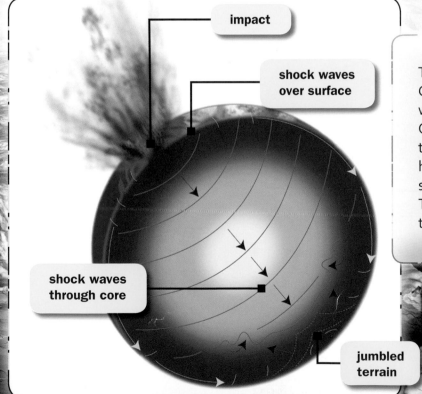

impact

shock waves over surface

shock waves through core

jumbled terrain

The impact that created Caloris sent shock waves through Mercury. On the other side of the planet, they caused huge earthquakes that shattered the surface. The area is known as the jumbled terrain.

WHAT TO SEE ON VENUS

Venus is covered with winding "rivers" and low-lying flood plains. They weren't formed by water, but by red-hot molten rock! The planet is packed with volcanic features you won't find anywhere else in the solar system.

Volcanoes

More than 1,000 major volcanoes dot the surface of Venus. Most are clustered together in small hilly areas called regio. Eistla Regio is a must-see for its pancake domes. You won't find these weird, flat lava domes anywhere else in the solar system.

Maat Mons and Sapas Mons are volcanoes named after goddesses from different cultures. Maat Mons is the tallest volcano on Venus. At 8 kilometres (5 miles) above average surface level, it's twice as high as the largest active volcano on Earth!

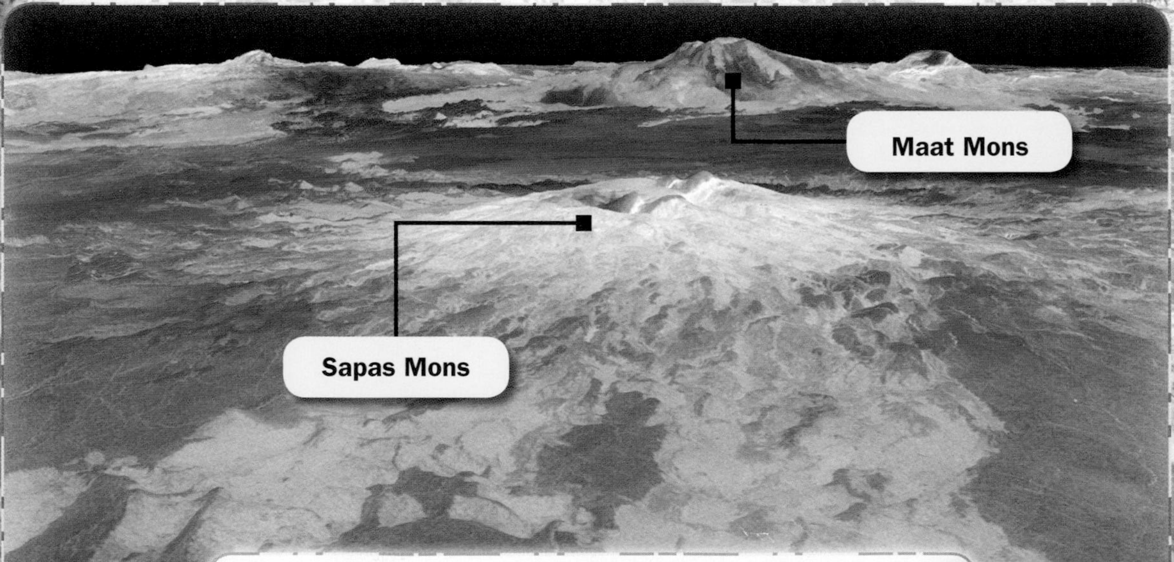

Maat Mons

Sapas Mons

A computer created this 3D view of Venus' surface, using information collected by probes.

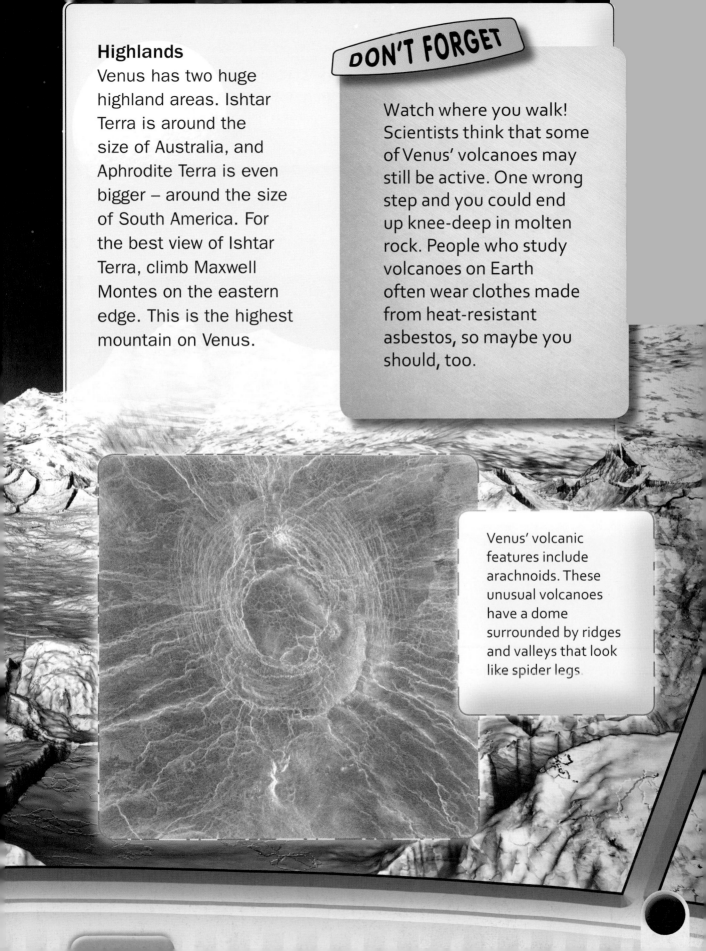

Highlands

Venus has two huge highland areas. Ishtar Terra is around the size of Australia, and Aphrodite Terra is even bigger – around the size of South America. For the best view of Ishtar Terra, climb Maxwell Montes on the eastern edge. This is the highest mountain on Venus.

DON'T FORGET

Watch where you walk! Scientists think that some of Venus' volcanoes may still be active. One wrong step and you could end up knee-deep in molten rock. People who study volcanoes on Earth often wear clothes made from heat-resistant asbestos, so maybe you should, too.

Venus' volcanic features include arachnoids. These unusual volcanoes have a dome surrounded by ridges and valleys that look like spider legs.

CRATER SPOTTING

Venus has far fewer craters than Mercury, and each one is more than 1.5 kilometres (2 miles) wide. The planet's thick atmosphere burns up small meteoroids before they can hit the surface. It also slows down any large meteoroids that do make it through, so the craters are wide but shallow.

Lava has filled in many craters. The thousand or so that are left are unlike any others in the solar system. Some have unusual features created by molten lava flowing out of the crater, such as the mermaid's tail of the Addams Crater.

Don't miss seeing the mermaid's tail of the Addams Crater when you visit Venus!

OTHER FEATURES

You will also come across coronae. These large "blisters" of rock were formed by hot magma rising up under the surface without breaking through. The biggest is Artemis Corona, which is 2,600 kilometres (1,600 miles) across.

WHO'S WHO?

Maxwell Montes is the only site on Venus named after a man, in honour of James Clerk Maxwell (1831–1879). He was a Scottish scientist who made very important discoveries about light. Most sights on Venus are named after famous women from history or myths. These include Guinevere, Cleopatra, and Aphrodite.

Molten magma oozed from cracks and created long, winding channels. From a distance they look like rivers hundreds of kilometres long.

INTERVIEW WITH AN ASTRONAUT

Paolo Nespoli is an Italian astronaut with the European Space Agency (ESA). He enjoys scuba diving, flying aeroplanes, and photography. In 2007, Paolo went into space for 15 days, and in 2010 he spent a further 6 months in space. In total, he has travelled more than 111 million kilometres (69 million miles).

Q *When you came back from the International Space Station, was it difficult to get used to not being weightless?*

A My first ride, which was considered a short duration flight, was fifteen days. Coming back, I really felt the effects of gravity pretty heavily, and so I was wondering how I would feel when I came back after six months. Now I know it's pretty bad. I felt I weighed two or three hundred kilograms. Just lifting my arm was something that I needed to do consciously and pay attention to it. I mean, I had a watch on and I felt the watch was weighing three kilos on my arm! Walking was very difficult, both because of the muscles [being weak], but also because of nausea, balance problems, all sorts of things like that.

Q Would you prefer to be weightless all the time, if you could?

A You learn after a while to float around like Spider-man, from one wall to another wall, just pushing yourself ... Of course, sometimes you misjudge the effort that it takes or the push that you push, so you go and slam into walls and other stuff. But this is part of the fun, I think. I find myself like a little kid, exploring, doing things in a different way. It was very nice to just float around, push here, push there, go here, go there, pick up something that weighs three, four, five hundred kilos, and just move it around like nothing.

On the other hand, it was really irritating that you can only handle two or three things, and then you start losing stuff. If you lose something, it doesn't go on the floor, it goes all around and it's difficult to find. It happened several times, I would be eating something – a little pouch with some food and a spoon – and suddenly the spoon is gone, or the food is gone! And two hours later you're passing by, and there is your spoon or your tuna floating right in the middle of the module!

Q If you were talking to a student, what would you tell them they need to really focus on learning if they want to be an astronaut?

A I'd tell them, "you need to understand what you like, what you will be good at. Something that you can do all day and not be tired of, and be happy with what you are doing." It's almost like finding out what is your nicest hobby or most precious hobby and make it your work, so you are paid to do a hobby, and at the end of the day you are happy and not tired. You really need to find what makes you happy and make it your profession. And if this is being an astronaut, please go ahead.

COULD HUMANS LIVE ON MERCURY OR VENUS?

Although robot probes and powerful instruments on Earth have investigated other planets, no human has ever been to another planet. Could astronauts visit or even live on Mercury or Venus one day?

It would be very difficult. Earth has the perfect conditions for life. There is water to drink, **oxygen** to breathe, and enough sunlight to keep us warm without getting too hot. Venus has a similar size and structure to Earth, but conditions are very different. Without special protection, an astronaut would be squashed by the atmosphere, prevented from breathing by the poisonous air, boiled by high temperatures, or dissolved by acid rain!

DON'T FORGET

The air on Venus is mainly carbon dioxide, which is toxic to humans. Traces of sulphur dioxide also make it stinky. Mercury has a tiny bit of oxygen but because the air pressure is very low, the oxygen is too widely spread out to breathe. So, on either planet you'll need air tanks for breathing.

Mercury does not have a proper atmosphere, so you won't have the same problems as on Venus. But that does not mean it is free of trouble. There is nothing to block the Sun's searing heat or radiation from space. It's not surprising that there are no signs of life on Mercury or Venus.

Even super-tough robot probes costing millions of dollars only survived for a few hours on Venus' surface. They were destroyed by the intense heat and pressure.

Scientists have coloured this picture of Venus to show the lower areas in blue, and the higher areas in green.

FUTURE EXPLORATION

Humans may not ever be able to live on Mercury and Venus, but that doesn't stop us from wanting to study them. Understanding the history and geology of these planets helps scientists to understand how Earth formed. It also helps them to hunt for planets near other stars in our galaxy.

ALL ABOARD FOR VENUS

Japan hopes that its *Akatsuki* probe will be the next spacecraft to orbit Venus. The probe arrived at the planet in 2010, but didn't slow down enough to enter orbit. Its next opportunity will come in 2016.

Once in orbit, *Akatsuki* will study Venus' thick clouds and look for active volcanoes.

BepiColombo will look out for asteroids close to the Sun.

NEXT STOP: MERCURY

The European Space Agency (ESA) will put a spacecraft into orbit around Mercury in 2019. *BepiColombo* will fly past Venus on its six-year journey to Mercury. Once it enters Mercury's orbit, it will study the planet for up to two years, answering questions about its structure, craters, magnetic field, and atmosphere. It will even look out for asteroids close to the Sun.

Each new mission to Mercury and Venus answers many questions, but brings big surprises and new mysteries too. What will you discover on your trip?

AMAZING FACTS

Some space trips are already being offered to the public. For several hundred thousand dollars, space tourists can zoom up to the edge of Earth's atmosphere for an astronaut's view of our planet.

MAP OF THE SOLAR SYSTEM

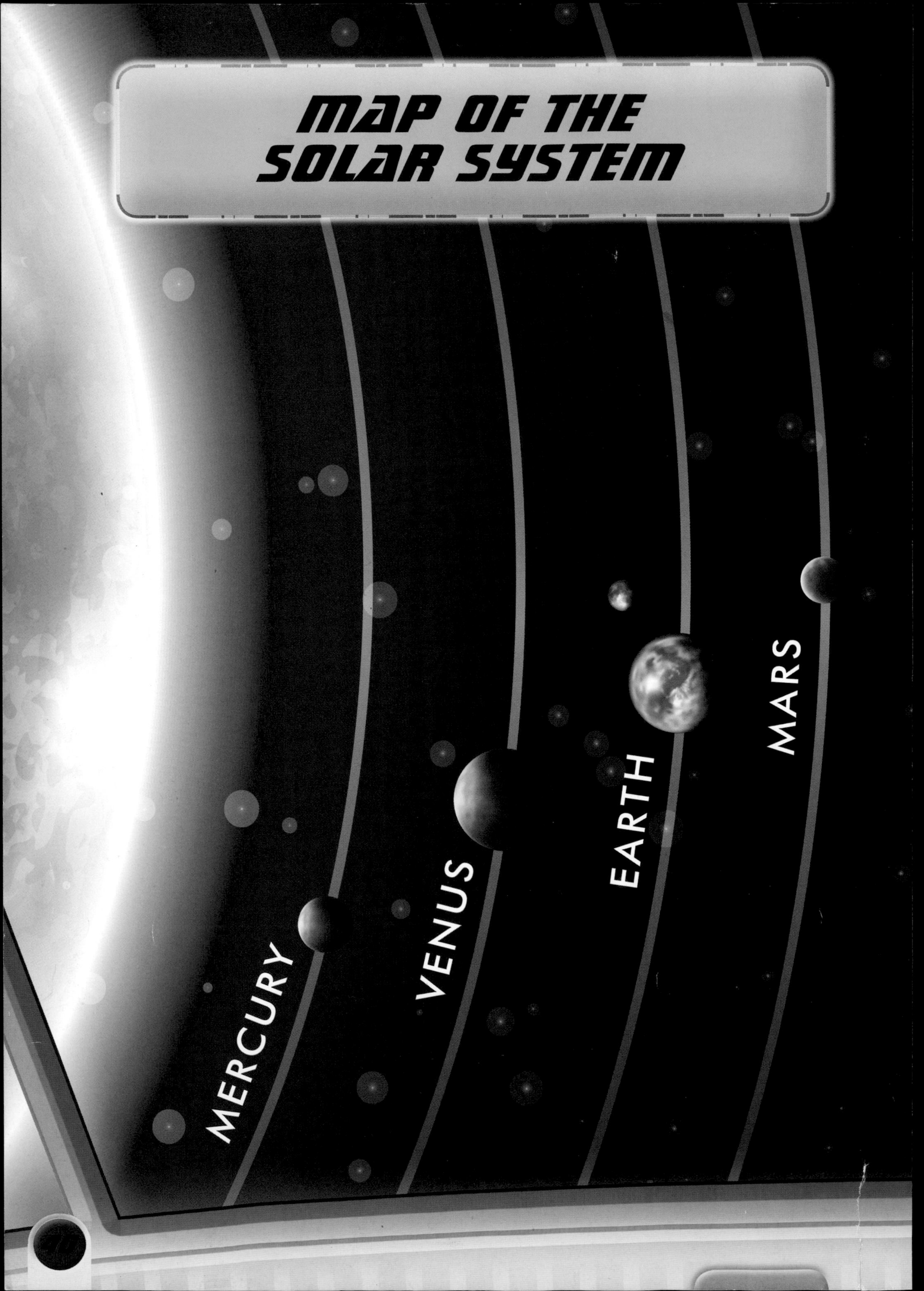

MERCURY

VENUS

EARTH

MARS

ASTEROID BELT

JUPITER

SATURN

URANUS

NEPTUNE

The sizes of the planets and their distances from the Sun are not to scale. To show all the planets' real distances from the Sun, this page would have to be about one kilometre long!

TIMELINE

c. 3500–500 BC Ancient Egyptians observed Mercury and Venus, and called Mercury "Thoth", after their god of knowledge.

733 BC Mayans record observation of Venus as a morning "star".

727 BC Mayans record observation of Venus as an evening "star".

c. 450 BC Ancient Greeks call Mercury two different names, Apollo (god of truth) and Hermes (messenger god of writing).

AD 650 Mayans create a calendar based on the changing position of Venus in the night sky.

1610 Galileo Galilei is the first person to observe Venus through a telescope.

1933 Eugenios Antoniadi makes the first map of Mercury's surface using a telescope.

1962 *Mariner 2* visits Venus and discovers how hot its surface is.

1965 Gordon Pettengill and Rolf Dyce use the Earth's *Arecibo* radio telescope to measure how fast Mercury spins.

1967 *Venera 4* enters Venus' atmosphere and discovers it is mainly made up of carbon dioxide.

1970 *Venera 7* lands on Venus and sends back data for 23 minutes before being destroyed by heat.

1974–1975 *Mariner 10* takes the first close up pictures of Mercury's surface, but can only photograph one side.

1981 *Venera 13* and *14* land on Venus and survive for 2 hours and 7 minutes. They send back colour photographs and data about the soil.

1991 Scientists based on Earth spot signs of ice in cold craters at Mercury's north and south poles.

2006 *Venus Express* goes into orbit around Venus.

2008 *Mercury Messenger* flies past Mercury and begins to send back photographs of Mercury, including the side that was not seen by *Mariner 10*.

2011 *Mercury Messenger* goes into orbit around Mercury to study it more closely, with enough fuel to stay until 2013.

FACT FILE

	Mercury	Venus	Earth
Diameter	4,875 km (3,029 mi.)	12,104 km (7,521 mi.)	12,756 km (7,926 mi.)
Average distance from Sun	58 million km (36 million mi.), like flying from London to Sydney 3,415 times	108 million km (67 million mi.), like flying from London to Sydney 6,349 times	150 million km (93 million mi.), like flying from London to Sydney 8,813 times
Surface temperature	−180°C to 430°C (−292°F to 806°F)	464°C (867°F)	15°C (59°F)
Air	52% oxygen 39% sodium vapour 8% helium 1% other gases (the total amount of air is extremely small in comparison to Earth's air)	96.5% carbon dioxide 3.5% nitrogen and other gases (traces of water vapour, sulphur dioxide, argon)	78.1% nitrogen 20.9% oxygen 1% other gases (argon and traces of other gases)
Gravity	0.38 of Earth's gravity	0.9 of Earth's gravity	1
What would I weigh if I weigh 61 kg (135 lbs) on Earth?	Mercury's gravity is around one third of Earth's gravity. This means that an astronaut's weight would also be around one third of his or her weight on Earth. For example, if you weigh 61 kg (135 lbs) on Earth, you will weigh just 23 kg (50 lbs) on Mercury.	Venus' gravity is only slightly less than Earth's gravity. This means that an astronaut would weigh slightly less than they do on Earth. For example, if you weigh 61 kg (135 lbs) on Earth, you will weigh 56 kg (123 lbs) on Venus.	61 kg (135 lbs)

GLOSSARY

asteroid small object in the solar system that is travelling on its own path around the Sun

astronomer person who studies space

atmosphere layer of gases surrounding a planet

axis (plural: **axes**) imaginary line that planets spin around

core central part of a planet

crater dish-shaped hole in the surface of a planet, made by a meteorite smashing into the surface

crust thin, rocky outer layer of a planet

data facts and statistics that have been collected

dissolve break down and become thoroughly mixed with a liquid

gravity force that pulls objects towards each other. Big objects, such as planets, have much stronger gravity than smaller objects, such as people.

instrument machine or tool for measuring something – for example, speed, temperature, or position

magnetic field region around a magnet where it has an effect on magnetic materials and other magnets

mantle area between the crust and core of a planet

meteoroid small piece of rock, metal, or ice orbiting the Sun

molten solid that has melted to become liquid

mythology stories and tales from ancient times, often involving heroic deeds and adventures

NASA National Aeronautics and Space Administration, the US space agency

observatory building with telescopes and other instruments for observing (looking at) stars and planets

orbit path of an object around a star or planet

oxygen gas needed by living things

particle very tiny object

pressure pushing force on an object from something touching it, such as the pushing force of the air on our bodies

probe robot spacecraft sent to visit planets, moons, and other objects in the solar system

radar system for "seeing" objects by sending out short bursts of radio waves, which bounce off the object

radiation particles and rays that come from some objects in space, such as stars. Some types of radiation are harmful to humans.

solar system the Sun, the planets, and other objects that are in orbit around it

Soviet Union name for an area of Asia and Eastern Europe that used to be one huge country, but is now made up of many separate countries

space agency organization involved in space research and exploration

sulphur dioxide poisonous and smelly gas made out of sulphur and oxygen

telescope device that makes distant objects look bigger

universe everything that exists, including all of space and all the objects and energy in it

FIND OUT MORE

BOOKS

Book of Astronomy and Space, Lisa Miles and Alastair Smith (Usbourne, 2009)

Space: A Children's Encyclopedia (Dorling Kindersley, 2010)

Space Blog, Angela Royston (A&C Black, 2012)

The Pop Up, Pull Out Space Book (Dorling Kindersley, 2010)

Wow! Space, Carole Stott (Dorling Kindersley, 2010)

WEBSITES

messenger-education.org
See the latest pictures taken by NASA's *Mercury Messenger* mission.

solarsystem.nasa.gov/eyes/index.html
Explore the solar system from the comfort of your own home using this amazing 3D interactive website.

solarsystem.nasa.gov/timeline/index.html
See who has explored space before you using this interactive timeline.

www.esa.int/SPECIALS/Venus_Express/index.html
Find out what Venus Express has discovered recently and watch some amazing animations of conditions on Venus' surface (click on "Animations" in the menu bar). You can even download instructions to cut out and build your own model of the Venus Express space probe!